CEREAL

TRAVEL & STYLE

SKAGEN

TOAST

TOA.ST

EDITOR'S LETTER

California is a place I find easy to love. With its fabled and varied natural beauty, year round agreeable climate, and ultra laid back lifestyle, the Golden State has long occupied a special place in my heart. I've often promised myself I would move there one day. My rose tinted view of Cali has intensified in recent years, though I have often wondered if that is simply down to the fact that I now reside over 5,000 miles away in rainy England. Distance does perhaps make the heart grow fonder. What if my next sojourn to Santa Barbara, Lake Tahoe, or San Francisco comes up short of my vaunted expectations? This was just one of the thoughts percolating in my mind as I landed in SFO back in April, bound for the Northern Californian adventure we had planned for this volume.

Those transient doubts evaporated the moment we began our drive down the historic State Route One towards Big Sur, zooming past strawberry and artichoke fields, over terrain covered in dusty pink heather and fragrant chaparral. Gliding along the asphalt curves hugging the 85 mile stretch of coast where the Santa Lucia Mountains dive into the Pacific Ocean, I was struck by the sheer scale of Big Sur and the glittering Pacific unfolding before us. This experience was followed by a vinous jaunt through Napa and Sonoma, where palm trees and powder blue skies frame immaculate vineyards, and Thomas Love Peacock's observation that "the juice of the grape is the liquid quintessence of concentrated sunbeams" never rings truer. Under the iridescent Californian sun in Sonoma County, vines glisten as they slope towards the ocean, in towns like Jenner, where the Russian River opens out to sea. Here, at a small cliff top restaurant called River's End, I encountered one of the most painterly sunsets I have ever seen; a horizon brushed with strokes of crimson and burnt sienna.

Over in Yosemite, comparable feelings of awe were awoken as I took in the soaring granite spires of Half Dome and El Capitán, the largest exposed granite monolith in the world. Hiking alongside sequoias that are thousands of years old, I imagined the wonder that John Muir, the great naturalist, must have felt when he walked these paths. I was prompted to purchase his seminal text, *The Yosemite*, in order to be better equipped next time, because, yes, I will return.

Creating this volume of *Cereal* has allowed me to reaffirm my love of California. I hope it will provoke similar feelings of warmth as you read our opening chapter.

Rosa Park

SAY HELLO

hello@readcereal.com

Cereal Magazine
Bristol & Exeter House
The Penthouse
Lower Station Approach
Temple Meads
Bristol BS1 6QS
United Kingdom

 *@cerealmag*

 */cerealmag*

 *@cerealmag*

COVER BY JUSTIN CHUNG

FIND US ONLINE

www.readcereal.com

ONLINE SHOP

www.readcereal.com/shop
sales@readcereal.com

BECOME A STOCKIST

stockist@readcereal.com

ADVERTISE WITH US

advertise@readcereal.com

Cereal is a bi-annual publication. The articles published reflect the opinions of the respective authors and do not necessarily represent the views of the publishers and editorial team.

Printed in the United Kingdom at *Hampton Printing Ltd*, on FSC certified uncoated paper.

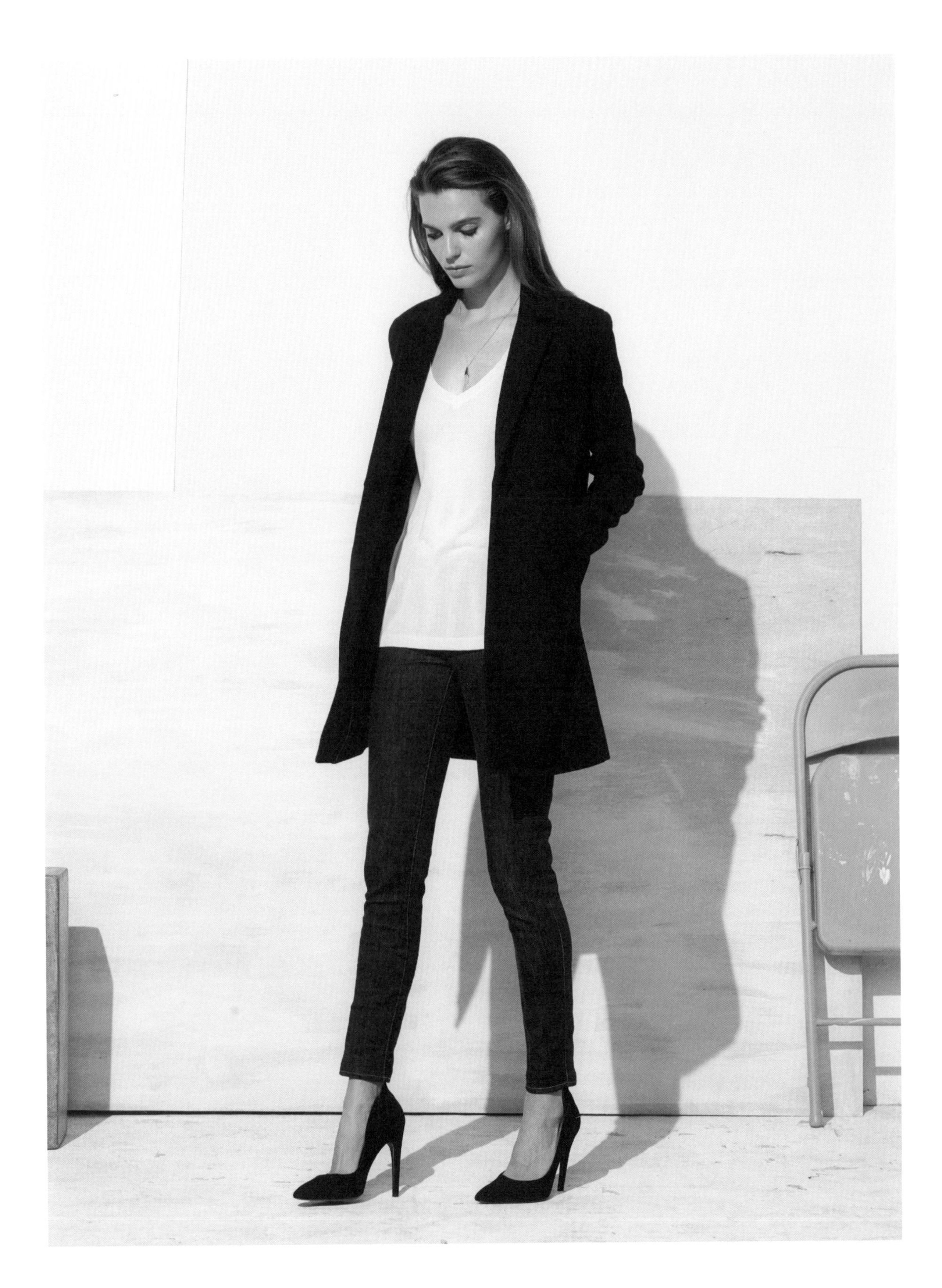

TABLE OF CONTENTS

N. CALIFORNIA, USA

Big Sur	*18*
24 hours	*28*
Heritage denim	*36*
Californian viticulture	*44*
Yosemite	*50*

ANTWERP, BELGIUM

Antwerp by DVN	*62*
Middelheim	*68*
Graanmarkt 13	*76*
Hands	*82*
Kanaal by Axel Vervoordt	*86*

INTERLUDE

CURATED: Timepieces	*98*
Vitsoe: Invisible design	*106*

A uniform vision 114

Agnes Martin 120

Haute horlogerie 128

Reading room 134

Artist series 142

PANAMA CITY, PANAMA

Panama canal 148

Casco Viejo 156

Soberanía National Park 164

CONTRIBUTORS

Adrienne Pitts
Alison Elwin
Anders Schonnemann
A. H. Lee
Carmen Chan
Chaney Kwak
Charlie Lee-Potter
Finn Beales
Jonathan Gregson
Justin Chung
Justin H. Min
Kate Holstein
Lilli Millhiser
Lily Le Brun
Line Klein
Lucy Brook
Mark Sanders
Nathalie Schwer
Sean Hotchkiss
Toby Mitchell

N. CALIFORNIA

USA

37°46’52.13”N 122°25’8.67”W

BIG SUR

CALIFORNIA DREAMING

Words: *Sean Hotchkiss* *Photos:* *Finn Beales*

BIG SUR'S ETHEREAL QUALITIES HAVE MADE IT AN ESCAPE FOR CREATIVE MINDS OVER THE LAST CENTURY; ARTISTS, WRITERS, RECLUSES, SELF SEEKERS – ALL HAVE COME HERE TO SHED THE RIGIDITY OF SOCIETY FOR A WHILE.

Big Sur doesn't exist in the way other places exist; no one knows precisely where it begins or ends. Its 145 km or so of coastline purportedly run from the Carmel River in Monterey County South to San Carpóforo Creek in San Luis Obispo, on California's northern coast. There is no centre of town. No Main Street. Every minute one spends within its expanses has a soft, dreamlike quality that begins to harden and crack the second you accelerate north towards the Bay Area and impending reality. Big Sur is a reverie. Appropriately enough, I was asleep the first time I arrived.

We had driven up from San Diego. Two friends from Texas and me. When I awoke in the backseat, it was to cries of "Pull over!" – a common occurrence along this particular stretch of the Monterey coastline, where every vista is seemingly superior to the last. So began my familiarity with the rites of those lucky souls who have travelled to this part of the West. We slept in a cabin smothered in dense trees on the forest side of Route One, and lived for two days on frozen pizzas, gas station coffee, and ripe fruit from the stands that line the Pacific coast. We manoeuvred our car along the snakelike stretches of Highway One for hours, stopping only for snacks, for gas, to use the bathroom – after which we passed a joint around and I slipped gently off again, only to wake to more cries of "Pull over!" Then came another beautiful handful of minutes spent standing on the edge of a mountainside, staring at the whirling, rhythmic sea below, my chest heaving from the sprint to the guardrail.

There is only one way to begin a day in Big Sur; with the silent sunrise. If you're fortunate, yours will be a morning when the thick fog rolls off the salty waves crashing down below the cliffs, swallowing much of the hillside and hanging around you like a hug. The fog might break momentarily, offering you flashes of rocky shore, flares of sunlight, and mossy bluffs. The air will smell sweet (like the kelp and foam down on the beach) and fragrant (like the eucalyptus and sage growing at your feet). Zombielike fellow travellers will have gathered in homage to observe alongside you. No one speaks. As the sun appears over the ocean, a bit of sadness creeps in. You know the rest of the day can't possibly be as beautiful. There will be the smoke from barbecue grills at roadside stops, the low rumble of elephant seals perched on rocky peninsulas, and the thin sand from winding trails ending up in your sneakers, but nothing will quite compare to that sunrise. Not for me, at least. As luck should have it, the same plump, orange orb will dip back below the Pacific that evening. One final firework.

▶▶▶

◀◀◀

Big Sur's ethereal qualities have made it an escape for creative minds over the last century; artists, writers, recluses, self seekers – all have come here to shed the rigidity of society for a while. The poetry of Robinson Jeffers and Henry Miller's *Big Sur and the Oranges of Hieronymus Bosch* are works that perhaps best capture the questions one invariably asks oneself when faced with such overwhelming (and potentially society challenging) natural beauty. According to Miller: "The ideal community, in a sense, would be the loose, fluid aggregation of individuals who elected to be alone and detached in order to be at one with themselves and all that lives and breathes."

Alone and detached works in Big Sur, sure, but that faraway feeling Miller speaks of also makes this place an ideal nest for romance. Standing for several nanoseconds at these heights, surrounded by towering pines, it's impossible to imagine this place wasn't shaped in reverence of (and as an accessory to) love. Surely many pairs have spent nights high above these cliffs, listening to the crashing waves below, bathed in starlight and feeling very far from the world they've left behind, if only for an evening. I experienced love of that kind here, too. A trip to Big Sur last January was bittersweet, emotionally supercharged by the waning days of a relationship I hated to see go. We left the road from Los Angeles late in the evening and rose, doggedly, at 05:30 to catch the sunrise the following morning. As the pre-dawn light approached no less than photographic nirvana, I snapped a shot of her I'd later caption with *First Road Trip of 2015*. It would also be our last. In the picture, she's turned towards me, hands in pockets, framed by low hanging clouds, the suggestion of a smile breaking across her face. Like all moments in Big Sur, this one was fleeting, trancelike, not meant for the outside world; trapped forever, here in this magical place. ■

POST RANCH INN

This page ROOM WITH OCEAN VIEW
Opposite SIERRA MAR RESTAURANT

postranchinn.com

24 HOURS

A SHORT GUIDE TO SF & OAKLAND

Words: *Justin H. Min* *Photos:* *Rich Stapleton & Justin Chung*

SIGHTGLASS

Brothers and co-owners Justin and Jerad Morrison opened Sightglass in 2011 after years in the speciality coffee industry. Their 650 m² flagship space in San Francisco's industrial SoMA neighbourhood houses the company headquarters, roaster, and coffee bar. They've since opened at other locations including the Mission District, and inside the Ferry building. In the Mission venue, the bright, inviting space features a ceiling constructed of heirloom redwood and intricate floor tiling.

3014 20th Street, San Francisco, CA, 94110

MARCH

Opening its doors to its Pacific Heights clientele in 2003, March offers high quality pieces for the kitchen, pantry, and table. Drawing inspiration from the San Francisco food scene and the paintings of Carrie Mae Smith, owner Sam Hamilton conveys a sense of history with each of the objects featured in his immaculate store, and exhibits an array of artwork throughout the space. With the recent installation of an AGA cooker, March now also hosts family style suppers.

3075 Sacramento Street, San Francisco, CA 94115

BOOK/SHOP

Conceived as an online operation, Book/Shop made the move to bricks and mortar in 2013 with a book lover's paradise on Temescal Alley. Alongside favourite editions, vintage furniture, and quirky artwork, the shop offers a brand new selection of 80 to 100 rare titles to explore and enjoy every few weeks. Every square metre of the space is crammed with a sense of wonder and appreciation for everything related to the gentle art of reading.

482 D 49th Street, Oakland, CA 94609

BAR TARTINE

Situated in the Mission District on Valencia Street's bustling restaurant row, Bar Tartine, by culinary duo Nick Balla and Cortney Burns, boasts an eclectic menu drawing inspiration from Japanese, Hungarian, Middle Eastern, and Nordic cuisine. With ever evolving tastes and featuring the finest local produce in season, Tartine Bakery's restaurant sibling prepares many of its own ingredients inhouse, including aged cheeses, spices, *koji*, and *bottarga*. They contribute to many of the restaurant's signature dishes, such as chilled plum soup with *noyaux*, and beef tartare on toast with *tonnato* sauce and dried beef.

561 Valencia Street, San Francisco, CA 94103

SONG TEA & CERAMICS

White walls, concrete floors, and warm maple make up the understated gallery space and tasting room of Sutter Street's Song Tea & Ceramics. The atelier's tea collections, carefully curated by owner Peter Luong, feature traditional, rare, and experimental tea from China and Taiwan. Their fine flavours are paired with handcrafted ceramics created by a select group of artisans from around the world.

2120 Sutter Street, San Francisco, CA 94115

MILL MERCANTILE

Mill Mercantile carries an impeccable selection of clothing, home goods, and accessories. Founded in 2012 as the female counterpart to menswear brand Unionmade, this Noe Valley boutique has built a reputation for its selection of international brands. With items from as far afield as Japan, France, and Finland, you can find the perfect pair of Chimala jeans, a crisp MHL shirt, a striking Satomi Kawakita ring, and a classic Sir Madam pitcher, all under one roof.

3751 24th Street, San Francisco, CA 94124

HERITAGE DENIM

A HISTORY OF LEVI STRAUSS

Words: *Chaney Kwak* *Photos:* *Justin Chung* *Model:* *James Smith at Wilhelmina*
Stylist: *Lilli Millhiser* *Studio:* *Drift* *Hair & Makeup:* *Mark at Judy Casey*
Digital Tech: *Spencer Wells* *Assistant:* *True O'Neill*

Once, on a road trip in Bavaria, I made a pit stop in Buttenheim, the kind of mediaeval town that pop-up storybooks imitate. I visited a white and blue timbered house that was now a small museum, dedicated to a man who was born and raised there. His formative years, from 1829 to 1847, were spent in this picturesque German town. When he left, he travelled as far west as he could, first to New York, then eventually on to San Francisco. He would forever change the way the world dresses; his name was Levi Strauss.

Levi Strauss & Co has its headquarters in the heart of San Francisco, and it couldn't be more different from its founder's humble birthplace. Inside the soaring atrium, awash in Californian sun, I browse vitrines containing an array of veteran denim from a tattered pair of jeans, once used to tow a car, to a blinged out jacket adorned with bottle caps and trinkets. This is The Vault, the lobby exhibition space of Levi's, and it is a crash course on the clothing conglomerate's corporate history, with displays such as Gold Rush era dungarees, photographs of denim clad WWII soldiers, and jeans worn by celebrities. This little showcase might as well be a tribute to the country's history at large, however; the story of denim is intricately intertwined with the modern history of the USA, the West, and specifically San Francisco. What else encapsulates this once scrappy city's spirit better than a pair of humble work pants, created by an immigrant for hard working labourers, reinvented continuously with the passing of time, and then exported across the globe?

Paul O'Neill, Head of Design at Levi's Vintage Clothing, is entrusted with bringing original designs from the archive back to life. Stitch by stitch, rivet by rivet, O'Neill revives garments that had been relegated to memory by replicating a few of the 20,000 historic items in the archives each year. "Today's fashion trends do not influence how we curate Levi's Vintage Clothing," O'Neill says, explaining that he actively tries to ignore current fads when deciding which items to resuscitate. "We are always digging into American history, looking for new stories to tell."

As I leave the Levi's building, I spot Coit Tower, a slim, 64 m Art Deco monument surrounded by boxy, two storey homes. Next, I walk up Filbert, a street so steep that at one point, it simply gives up, turning into a set of wooden steps scaling Telegraph Hill toward the tower. The stairs zigzag under a canopy of gnarled trees, and then through terraced gardens where the air is scented with honeysuckle. Far above the noise of the streets, the only sounds I hear belong to a flock of feral parrots that have found their home here. Like most San Franciscans, these red masked parakeets are descendants of migrants from elsewhere; originally from the Andes, it's likely they came to the city as pets before taking to the wild again. From the tower, I watch San Francisco shimmer through the recurrent fog that has begun rolling in. The enigmatic Transamerica Pyramid soars through the translucent curtain, flanked by anonymous grey skyscrapers. With one hand I block them out; right beneath my palm are pastel hued Victorian houses dating to the late 19th century, and I am reminded of O'Neill's words about digging into history in order to tell new stories. Orienting oneself to the past to create a brand new story today had sounded like an oxymoron – especially in the context of this tech boomtown where a youthful workforce devote their lives to building the newest, shiniest gadgets – but looking down at the city unfurling beneath me like a quilted blanket, his comments make sense. From a trading post of the Muwekma Ohlone people to a Spanish mission, a Gold Rush port to tech epicentre, the city has come a long way. Despite the trappings of a hypermodern technopolis, San Francisco is still an old fashioned town at heart. ■

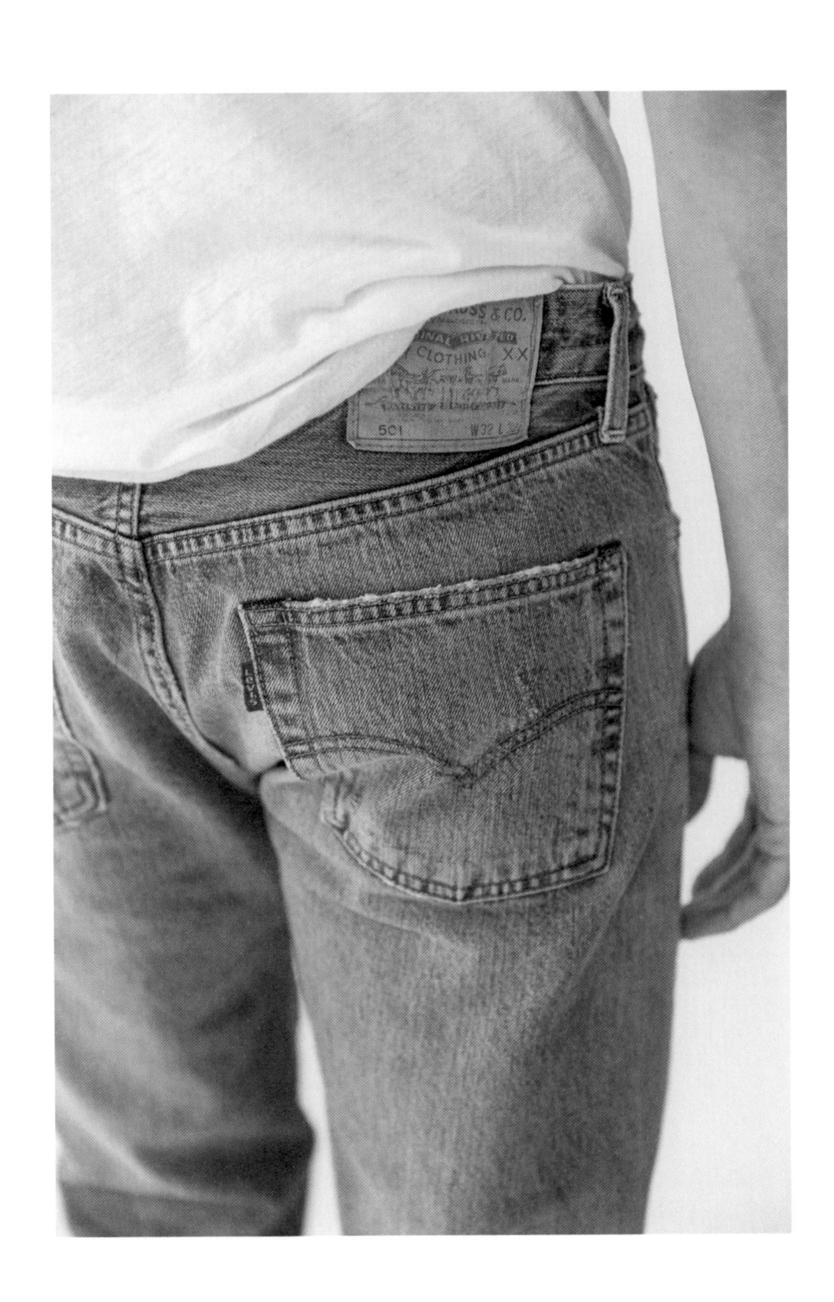
CLOTHING XX
501

Remington
QUIET-RITER
SCRIBE.
RIESLING

CALIFORNIAN VITICULTURE

MODERN WINEMAKING WITH SCRIBE

Words: Chaney Kwak Photos: Rich Stapleton

Whatever stereotypical image the Californian wine country may conjure up for you – tipsy folks your parents' age, perhaps, stumbling from one stuffy tasting room manned by snobby sommeliers to another – forget it. When you get to Scribe, a Sonoma vineyard challenging all the rules of winemaking, you'll find a different picture altogether. Skinny palm trees tower over sun soaked hills lined with ripening vines, leaving no doubt that you're in California. Scattered about the grounds are weather beaten *haciendas*, some as old as the state itself, where you might happen upon a dinner party thrown by the likes of Bar Tartine chefs, or a movie being projected onto a whitewashed wall. Andrew Mariani, one of the two brothers behind Scribe, is the picture of today's gentleman farmer; easygoing in plaid, and eloquent as a poet in his descriptions. Driving his dented Chevy Silverado down the winery's unpaved driveway, he spoke with *Cereal* about his eight year old passion project's past and future.

What was the inspiration behind Scribe?

My brother Adam and I both got interested in viticulture in college, and I ended up majoring in international trade and winemaking. When I returned to California eight years ago, after working for wineries in Europe, I got talking to an uncle who lived in Sonoma County. We were cruising around when we happened upon the property that would become Scribe. It was an abandoned, rundown place that used to be a turkey farm. We later found out that it was originally a winery, until Prohibition put an end to it. I went to libraries to piece together its history, and the more I learned, the more it steered me in the direction that Scribe would take. For instance, instead of the Pinot and Chardonnay that tend to dominate the area today, we planted Riesling and Silvaner, the first vines to be grown in the area.

How does history influence your work?

Relatively speaking, Scribe is a new winery, but it has roots reaching back to the Wild West. There are three very old buildings remaining on the property, including our office, a place I live in, and a *hacienda* that dates back to the 1850s. We're renovating the *hacienda* to host tastings and dinners. It should be ready by the end of 2015. In 2007, Scribe's first year, we spent almost the entire 12 months just demolishing old barbed wire fences and sheds. That time was really crucial. I uncovered a lot of history in the form of old things like bottles, foundations, and stone walls with aqueducts inside them that still run with water when it rains. While pulling poison oak and berry bushes, we found glass vials. I did some research and learned that there were a dozen Chinese workers who lived in the ravine in the 1880s – they were the ones who tended the vines back then – the vials turned out to be opium containers. Sure, winemaking comes from Europe, but being on a property that is so rooted in Californian history, we let that inspire what we do rather than taking our cues from other parts of the world.

SCRIBE

How would you describe Scribe's wine?
We have deep, volcanic soils and proximity to maritime breeze. The terroir is mineral rich, salty, and airy. It's a refreshing, bright environment, and you can see that reflected in some of the wine. We grow Silvaner, which is pretty rare in California. It's particularly vibrant, and I want to see that liveliness reflected in everything we do.

What makes Californian winemaking distinct?
I don't think Californian wine as a whole can even be defined yet. Can we say there is such a thing as Californian terroir? We're still such a young state – we only became part of the USA in 1850 – and it's also a vast area. The same goes for Californian cuisine; using local, seasonal, fresh produce is essential here, but beyond that, we're constantly progressing. I've been reading a lot of old Californian magazines that were basically about teaching people how to live in the West, and I see a lot of Mexican fingerprints. A lot of people talk about the Mediterranean influences in Californian cuisine and wine, but you can't forget that this used to be part of Mexico. While I was in Mexico City recently, I had dinner at Contramar. It was phenomenal, so I invited chef Gabriela Cámara to come up to cook. She took a walk around the vineyards, and found an old agave plant. She harvested it, pulled the fibrous outer layers off, dried them out, and cooked fish and chiles in them. She served agave spears over them along with 2013 Chardonnay, Riesling, and rosé.

How does food figure into your work as a vintner?
Wine can seem like a very serious thing, but when it comes down to it, we're farmers who grow fruit and ferment it. Wine shouldn't be put on a pedestal. We owe it to ourselves to celebrate everything that comes with it; the taste, the beautiful environment, the ambiance. As winemakers, we create something unique. It's a wonderful thing. We bring people together to communicate and celebrate. We try to strip away all the bullshit and offer straightforward dinners that are honest and simple. Some people see us as all young and hip – which, admittedly, we do have a lot of – but whenever we have dinners here, we see little kids, old dudes, and all sorts of folks who come in especially from San Francisco. Anybody can join the Scribe Viticultural Society – that's the only criteria for getting guaranteed allocations of small batch wines and invitations to the events.

Why does community figure so prominently into your work?
As a producer, I find that the most rewarding thing is to communicate with the people who taste the end result. I was just 24 when I started out on this project. I was so enraptured with the process of figuring out how to start a winery, but I was also naïve and inexperienced. I was really into learning, and wanted to share my progress. A lot of wineries seem to want to hide what's really going on in their cellars, but I wanted to be as transparent as possible. I have a lot of members who are knowledgeable, and it was so cool to learn from them, and experiment. Pretending that we knew everything from day one seemed ridiculous. Wine and food are avenues for communication and community. It's such a human way of interacting with the world. My brother and the whole crew all have a lot of love for this place. We're just so stoked to share what we're doing. ■

2300 Napa Road, Sonoma, CA 95476
SCRIBEWINERY.COM

YOSEMITE

POETIC NATURE

Words: *Richard Aslan* ***Photos:*** *Jonathan Gregson*

Wide avenues, half full parking lots, and low buildings under bright advertising hoardings disappear behind us in the rear view mirror. The road curves up between russet hills, low scrub clings to sliding dust, and sparse saplings stagger up to rounded summits. Inclines steepen, scorched grass nudges at the carriageway, and trunks like fists anchor twisted trees to treacherous dirt. Higher still, whispering canopies lean in over the sunbaked tarmac as foliage darkens and thickens. Pines spike at white laced blue. A hissing membrane of water is torn, green and grey, into ropes of foam beside the road, drumming over chunks of granite in all shapes and sizes like the assembled skulls of a menagerie. Around a curve, slopes tip suddenly skywards, jutting into titanic teeth, broken and grey. On foot now, we cross a wooden walkway slung between stone pylons, the river beneath heaving and rolling in a muscular sheet. We follow the flow as it narrows to swift green glass over yellow sand, and a broad path plunges into a cathedral of vertical lines. Umber streaks over sienna, stabs of verdigris dapple dry swipes of viridian, bold gunmetal tumbles over bullhide. A thread of silver frays far above, painting the wall of rock dark, sowing the air with mist. At the summit, trees wriggle their toes into cracks between liquid slabs of rock, and the sky is scrubbed clean. The thin air is populated with dreams of flying. As close to the edge as I dare, I rock, once, twice, onto the balls of my feet. I imagine pushing myself into the vault of blue, over mountains stretching to the horizon like rumpled bolts of midnight velvet.

▶▶▶

◀◀◀

Facts about Yosemite National Park

- Yosemite National Park covers 3,026 km^2 of Tuolumne, Mariposa, and Madera counties in central eastern California.
- This uninterrupted chunk of the western Sierra Nevada ranges from 640 m to almost 4,000 m above sea level. Its highest point is Mount Lyell.
- The park contains 1,300 km of hiking trails and 560 km of roads.
- Over four million visitors came to Yosemite in 2014. The majority never left the confines of the 13 km long Yosemite Valley which accounts for just one percent of the park's overall area. In July 2011, almost 21,000 visitors came to Yosemite Valley in one day.
- The 1864 *Yosemite Grant*, signed by Abraham Lincoln, was the first document to protect land as a park in the USA. It paved the way for the country's first national park, Yellowstone, in 1872.
- Threatened by logging and overgrazing, Yosemite was turned over to federal jurisdiction in 1906, and to the newly formed National Park Service in 1916.
- 95% of the park is now designated as Yosemite Wilderness, protected against development, artificial disruptions, and traffic congestion.
- The park contains three groves of ancient Sequoia; Mariposa Grove (200 trees), Tuolumne Grove (25 trees), and Merced Grove (20 trees).

▶▶▶

Yosemite Landforms

The Sierra Nevada is a chunk of ancient igneous rock, torn from its mooring on a tectonic fault line and tilted gradually upwards over the last four million years. Durable granite, formed from solidified magma and shot through with quartz and feldspar, dominates the landscape. Successive outpourings from deep within the earth's crust have been shaped by sun, wind, and water into plunging cliffs, soaring peaks, and monumental domes. U-shaped valleys, waterfalls, moraines, and polished plateaux, are testament to Yosemite's glacial past. Particularly characteristic of Yosemite is the process of exfoliation, where expanding granite rocks, formed under great pressure deep underground, burst through surface layers. The resulting curves create the landscapes of North Dome, Half Dome, and the serpentine flow of Cloud's Rest. ■

ANTWERP

BELGIUM

51°13’10.0”N, 4°24’08.9”E

ANTWERP BY DVN

A TOUR OF THE CITY WITH DRIES VAN NOTEN

Words: *Lily Le Brun* ***Photos:*** *Rich Stapleton & Toby Mitchell*

Top COPYRIGHT BOOKSHOP
Bottom HOTEL JULIEN

CITIES ALWAYS CHANGE, BUT HERE IN ANTWERP, THERE IS BARELY A SINGLE STREET THAT DOES NOT EVOKE STRONG AND HAPPY MEMORIES FOR ME.

It's impossible to untangle the city of Antwerp from the life and work of Dries Van Noten. The 57 year old fashion designer was born here and it remains his base. His father was the proprietor of one of Antwerp's first upmarket fashion boutiques, and his own flagship store, Het Modepaleis – a five storey former department store – has helped transform Nationalestraat into one of the city's chicest neighbourhoods. Van Noten studied at the city's prestigious Royal Academy of Fine Arts, becoming a member of the lauded group of graduates known as the Antwerp Six. "We don't want to become a little Paris", he said in an interview shortly after graduating, "we want to stick to Antwerp and keep our own image and spirit." At a time when many successful fashion companies have been absorbed into larger luxury conglomerates, Van Noten has remained resolutely independent, and has maintained sole creative and financial control ever since launching the first collection 30 years ago. Equally, in a world where brands are ever more diffuse, garments continue to be the main focus of his business, with shoes and accessories remaining very much in a supporting role. Incredibly, Van Noten has chosen to never advertise. Instead, he channels his funds and creative energies into his four *prêt à porter* collections – two for women and two for men – that he restricts himself to each year. This notable autonomy is also evident in Van Noten's aesthetic; his fabrics are complicated and luxurious, his colours rich and unusual. Inspiration, like the materials themselves, comes from far and wide; fabric woven in Uzbekistan appears alongside high tech material from Japan, digital prints of cityscapes are juxtaposed with botanical drawings. For his most recent menswear collection, Van Noten chose to work with archetypes, adroitly manipulating *cliché* and *Kitsch*. Palm trees, leopard print, tartan, and images of Marilyn Monroe all found their way onto silken fabrics and suit jackets, creating a look that was both characteristically modern and unambiguously unique.

When *Cereal* caught up with Van Noten, it became clear that despite these diverse influences, Antwerp continues to be a touchstone for the designer. The spirit of the city is woven through the fabric of every collection.

▶▶▶

◂◂◂

Is this still the same city you grew up in?
Antwerp has obviously changed hugely, but its DNA remains the same. I do not have as much time as I would like to hang out in the city anymore, but whenever I drive through its streets, there is always something that sparks a memory. Whether it's an old restaurant where I used to have dinner, or a cafe I went to after class. Cities always change, but here in Antwerp, there is barely a single street that does not evoke strong and happy memories for me.

What's your earliest memory of Antwerp?
I remember being in my father's shop, the time I spent there observing clients, and somehow learning the job. It was a place I enjoyed spending time as a boy, so I learned things almost by osmosis, by just being around all the action and not with any conscious effort. I was lucky enough to learn the ways of this industry and how it works from a much younger age than most. That's when my love affair with fabrics began – with the way they fall, and the way they feel. The most exciting moment for me was accompanying my parents on trips to Paris and Milan for their shows, just to see the spectacle of it all.

What has kept you here in the city you grew up in?
I have travelled a lot, and I like discovering new cultures. I think there's something unique about every city I have been to, but Antwerp will always be home. This is where I decided to build my company and my first store. This is where my life is. To remain at home in an environment I understand, and with the support system it offered me, seemed natural. I am more than happy with that choice.

What is unique about Antwerp?
Its people, its history, its mercantile flair, its culture, its evolution, its fashion. And its size; Antwerp is just big enough to have everything you need, and thanks to the harbour, it has always had an international dimension. Even today, we have a great wealth of merchants here – sartorial flair often needs a generous budget! ■

Dries Van Noten's Top 10:

Ganterie Boon
Bakkerij Goossens
Philip's Biscuits
Cogels Osylei
Museum Plantin-Moretus
Het Bos, Ankerrui
Hotel Julien
Copyright Bookshop
Axel Vervoordt Kanaal
Dôme Restaurant

Top GANTERIE BOON
Bottom PHILIP'S BISCUITS

MIDDELHEIM

A DAY AT THE SCULPTURE PARK

Words: *Richard Aslan* *Photos:* *Rich Stapleton*

Anarres, Eriador, Archenland, Earthsea, Oz, Middelheim; a border post, flamingo pink, marks our entry point into this country, a single column sucking the ceiling down through the floor. The circular glass booth is empty, lightbulbs flashing weakly against a blue sky. There is no guard to stamp our passports or rifle through our luggage. No one to slump in the midday heat smoking contraband cigarettes. The wilderness beyond is flat and open, the sun beating down on tussocky earth. Someone has dreamed up a sheltering canopy, but until it matures, ants crawl over bald patches in the overlong grass. A sign in a language neither of us speaks is spiked into the ground; *Keep off the Grass!* Or perhaps; *Picnic Area.* Or maybe; *Danger – Landmines!* This is a buffer zone, a colony, a place in the making. Settlers come on the promise of overflowing breadbaskets and chubby infants, only to find stars shining through the holes in the barracks roof and wolves howling on the horizon. Cross country, we decide, and with a deep breath we leave the path, picking our way across uneven terrain, seed heads sticking to our sleeves. We meet a boulder, squatting tank sized, wrapped in bandages, and painted a dull, thick gold. We duck under the eaves of an unfinished tower, cheap brick shattered, yellow foam blossoming in the gaps beneath the window frames.

The Wilderness peters out at a fork in a path between an owl and an eagle, silent claws on plinths of bronze. We turn right through an archway of dark leaved rhododendrons. The air is moist, the hum of insects replaced by the silence of interrupted conversations. The remains of an army is scattered across the battlefield, frozen in defeat. Achilles, or Ulysses perhaps, his foe long flown, braces a heroic foot on an outcrop to draw his bow. Muscles pause mid tremble. A satyr gyres skyward, brandishing silent pipes in a call for aid that never came, a gorgon writhes on the lawn, her blue skin irresistible to a banquet of flies. A dancer throws her breasts to the skies, open mouthed, and emptied of movement. Renoir, ossified, Rogiers, petrified, a dead spider upturned in the courtyard of a rusting iron seraglio. A tractor chews up sticks and pinecones as it weaves its way towards us. We feed the jackdaws crumbs from our lunchboxes until the crows come and chase them away. I squint at a knot of figures under the pergola, daring them to move.

A wall of whispering foliage separates us from a chequerboard province of napkins, tables, and wrought iron chairs. Purses and lipsticks spill from unattended handbags. A duck and her husband waddle past a finger painted thatched cottage, a glasshouse stuffed with books, and a stillwater miasma over the hump of a bridge. This is the Old Country. As a goose watches her brood beside water the colour of olives, we collect maps to the Outer Regions, ice creams, and coffee, and traverse the meadow rising plumply from the white lime walls of the manor house. Two sisters stand in silent debate, the crests of their pregnant bellies all but touching. A congregation of silver chairs sit empty under a monkey puzzle tree, forgotten by the wedding party, gone to listen

▸▸▸

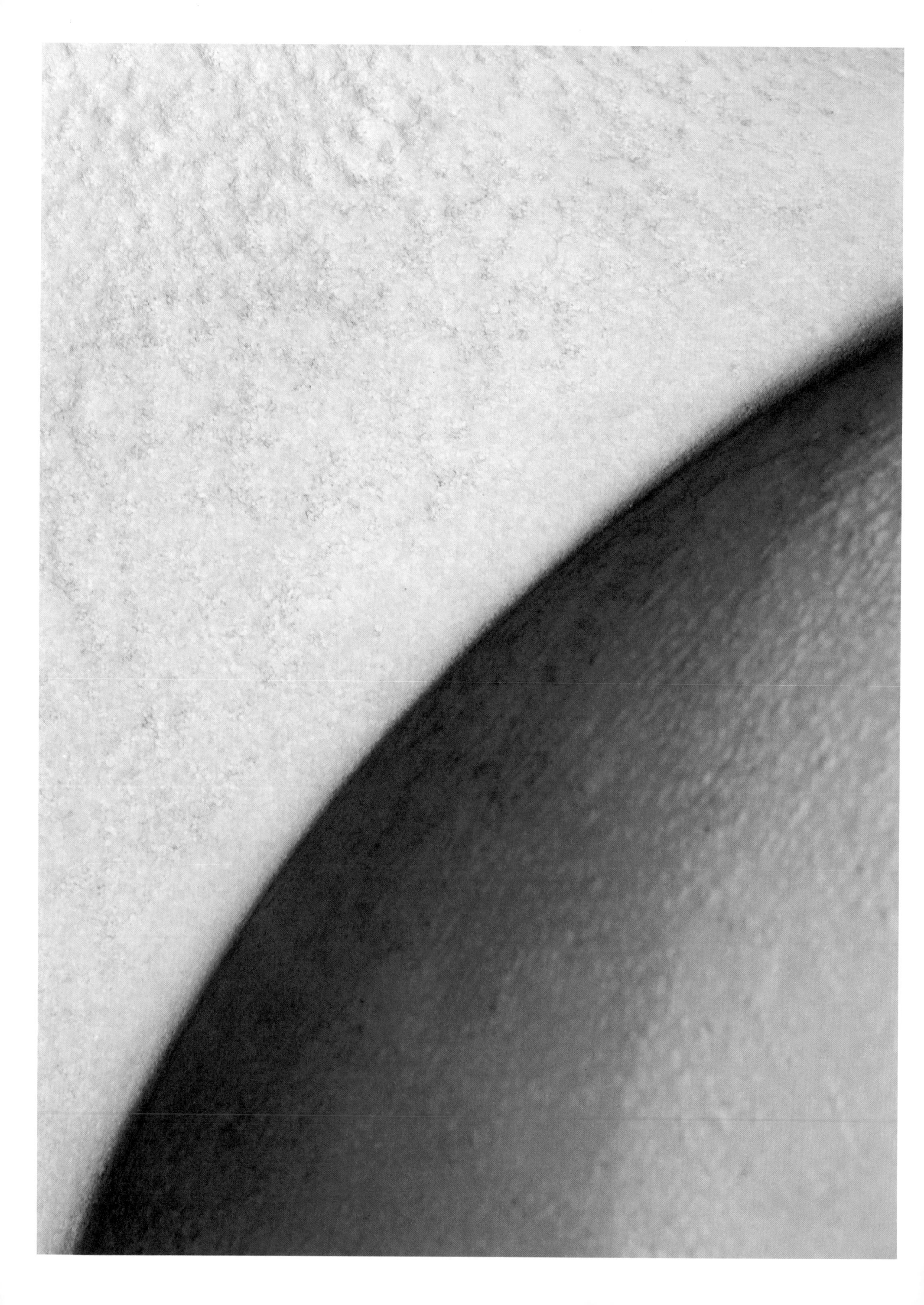

◀◀◀

to speeches and tryst under the willows. Statuary clusters, name plates, dates, pedigree, curve, mass, likeness, counterpoint. My mind quivers and I click my camera in the vain hope of taking at least some of it in. A light aircraft gnat buzzes overhead, skin stretched over ribs, armpit wings, a scatter of beechnuts across the ground. A shrouded captive, knife slashes in her blindfold, relaxes like an extra from a horror movie on a cigarette break. A skeleton high wire cycles through the treetops over an overturned Peugeot 205, dried mud handprints on the inside front passenger window. Disembodied cowls loom at one another, ghoulishness drained from them by the beams of sunlight and the traffic sucking at the perimeter fence.

There is a valley; bustle, bright orange coveralls, and tools spiking from a wheelbarrow. We inspect the pavilion under its billow of a roof as workers arrange rocks on the bed of a dry pond. "Is it too big for us?" I ask, squinting past cupped hands to swaddled plinths and ladders resting against walls. Thick slices of light spill over tiled floors like paint. "Not if we share it," he replies. In the forest beyond, a tall figure loiters, jaw against pelvis in shock at the slim golden boat it has drunkenly wrapped around a birch trunk. I recoil from a slim monolith of burnished silver, gnawed chunks revealing nose, lip, chest, the ticklish skin of a heel. The sun vanishes behind a cloud.

Waiting woods yield to grid, sliproad, and bark stripped saplings locked in looping plastic. Ideas congeal on cubes, more red than International Orange, two shades more cyan than Klein Blue. A thicket of girders bristles with manliness. A coppice of steel spikes glower at the real thing. On a cracked slab dusted with gravel, defrocked dignitaries avert their eyes from one another's fall from grace. Robbed of their pedestals, they are lumpen, fingers too big for their buttons. A functionary watches us from the window cut in her slanting shipping container, teachers scold their fluorescent flock, cars weave like somnolent cattle. The air thickens to gelatine as we cross an invisible line into the Enchanted Forest. With each step, the sense of being at the heart of it quickens, a spring winding itself ever tighter. Thoughts solidify, thick and fast, from the undergrowth; a blinded brick castle lying in wait to capture a princess; headless gymnasts marching crotch to buttock past *sudoku* columns; nodding donkeys tugging at stands of copper beech. Provinces nest one inside the other, ever smaller, interleaving and overlapping. Sculpted hills rear like velvet pillows, an emerald palace snares saplings in trellised traps, box hedges hem bamboo explosions, ski slopes, crushed barrels. A gilded chair faces a sheer brick wall.

The bench where we rest huddles in the scoop of a shivering bank of purple blossom. "I suppose the bees are more interested in the flowers than us?" he asks, worry creasing the spot between his eyebrows. I nod, sip blood warm water from my flask. We read a chapter or two of worms and witches, sand and spice, blue in blue eyes and bloated barons, aloud to the stillness, fortifying ourselves for the journey back out to the edges. There will be other adventures awaiting us; in every country of the imagination, getting to the centre is just the beginning. ■

Middelheim Open Air Sculpture Museum, Middelheimlaan 61, 2020 Antwerp

MIDDELHEIMMUSEUM.BE

GRAANMARKT 13

A CONCEPT LIFESTYLE

Words: Rosa Park Photos: Rich Stapleton

Housed in a historic, whitewashed townhouse on a tree lined square in the city centre, Graanmarkt 13 is designed in the signature Brutalist style of Belgian architect Vincent Van Duysen. Softened by the generous use of natural materials in muted tones, this multipurpose space – featuring a concept store, restaurant, gallery, and rental apartment – has a warmth and effortless style. We can't help but wish that we could move in and call it home. Conceived and run by husband and wife team Tim Van Geloven and Ilse Cornelissens, Graanmarkt 13 is understated in its disposition, a true paean to contemporary Belgian design.

Graanmarkt 13, 2000 Antwerp
GRAANMARKT13.BE

HANDS

LEGEND MEETS HISTORY

Words: *Richard Aslan* *Photos:* *Rich Stapleton*

A crag of greened bronze and stone rises from the Grote Markt outside the Stadhuis. Sea lions, serpents, and mermaids surge from the foam, bearing a ship that in turn bears a fort. On its battlement is a naked man, face and trunk streaked as though with copious tears, muscles twisting. Strain he might; the stately flow of the Scheldt lies three streets distant over the narrow stepped roofs of the Guildhalls, and the thing he would hurl into it is ungainly. Silvius Brabo, beloved of Caesar, grips the severed hand of the slain giant Druon Antigoon. A broken arc of water spurts from the wrist in lieu of blood, spattering the tourists below. This hand throwing – *hand werpen* in Flemish – is, as any daughter or son of the town will tell you, how Antwerp got its name.

Antigoon built his keep on the banks of the Scheldt, exacting half the burden of every passing craft, and cutting the hands from those who could or would not pay, throwing them into the swirling water. In Brabo's parting of flesh from bone, the defeated giant's hand became emblematic of the free waterway and the wealth it brought with it. Free trade made the Duchy of Brabant (also named for the hand throwing Roman) rich. By 1500, Antwerp was not only the wealthiest city in Europe, but also at the heart of a newly globalised world. Hundreds of ships bearing gold, silver, spices, fine cloth, and treasured hardwood, brought in many times more income for the city's Spanish masters than the American colonies combined.

By the end of the century, however, hands were wrung in despair at an unending parade of woes; 80 years of war, slaughter by rampaging Spanish infantrymen, religious rioting, plague, and the bankruptcy of the Spanish crown. In 1585, Antwerp's fate was sealed when a new giant, the Dutch Empire, closed the river. It is a token of the ruin wrought by the blockade that the citizenry plunged from 125,000 in the 1500s, to just 40,000 by the time of

▶▶▶

◀◀◀

Napoleon's precipitous rise in 1804. The emperor of the French saw in Antwerp the potential of a challenge to the growing power of London, and Bonaparte Dock was finished by 1811. His dreams of a new Europe crumbled, however, amid cannon smoke and musket fire in a field outside Waterloo, one Sunday in 1815. Instead, Antwerp became a battleground in the struggle for Belgian self rule. When the Siege of Antwerp ended in 1832, the freedom of the Scheldt became a banner for the fledgling Belgian state. It is no coincidence that Jef Lambeaux chose Brabo as the subject for his 1887 fountain, marking the lifting of the Dutch toll and the flow of the proceeds of free trade back into the city's coffers. The new century saw countless hands busy themselves in narrow houses on even narrower streets, in workshops and dockyards, cutting diamonds, hewing stone, and sewing hems, as Antwerp's prosperity blossomed.

The outbreak of the Great War made Antwerp once more a battlefield. The German army took the city in 11 days and held it until Armistice, setting the streets ablaze as they left. In picking up the pieces, the legend of Brabo reared its head again in 1934, when baker Jos Hacker created *Antwerpse handjes*, sweet, hand shaped biscuits baked and packed to a strict patent at the behest of the Royal Society of Master Confectioners. Respite was short, and from 1940 to 1944, horror rained once more on the city and its large Jewish community. Even liberation brought little relief as the retreating *Wehrmacht* pounded more V-2 missiles into its harbours than all its other wartime targets combined. From the rubble, a new Antwerp rose, slowly and painfully, rebuilt and reimagined on the same footprint of winding lanes. Modern houses were slotted in alongside brick and oak smoothed by the centuries. While diamonds and cargo remain, hands have also busied themselves with new trades. Since the 1990s, bright workrooms produce garments, realising the dream of squaring up to not only London, but also Milan, Paris, and New York. Trade in ideas has seen a parade of cultural institutions such as Rubens House Museum, Wide White Space Gallery, M HKA, the Fotomuseum, and MAS, rise between marketplaces and clattering trams. As a reminder of the journey back to prosperity, Antigoon's hand clusters on doorknobs, clothing labels, city maps, and chocolate shops. No matter that some etymologists claim that Antwerp really derives from *An 't Werf* - 'On the Wharf'; it is the way of legends to be truer than history. ■

KANAAL

BY AXEL VERVOORDT

Words: *Lucy Brook* *Photos:* *Rich Stapleton*

According to Axel Vervoordt, revered Belgian designer and antique collector, decoration is about more than just decorating. "My taste is dominated by a sense of proportion. I want to achieve a feeling of harmony between architecture, furnishings, works of art, and antiques." His organic approach, characterised by a commitment to fusing objects with their surroundings, respecting existing environments, and acknowledging the passage of time, has cemented Vervoordt's place in the firmament of design pioneers. He began working as an art and antiques dealer in the late 1960s, and one of his earliest projects was the painstaking restoration of 16 Renaissance houses in the Vlaeykensgang in Antwerp. A portion of this space was transformed into his home, and also the place from where he sold his treasures. He and his wife May travelled to antiques fairs across the world, first investing in collectables, and then expanding their shared passion into an interior and furniture design business, fuelled by a belief that each room has its own intrinsic character. Demand for their sofas and club chairs quickly mushroomed, and these items have remained staples of the Axel Verwoordt *Home Collection* ever since. His most iconic work remains residential, with a portfolio including Robert de Niro's Tribeca penthouse, and the homes of rockstars and royalty.

Despite an appreciation for beauty going back to his childhood, Vervoordt is adamant that his work isn't rooted in aestheticism, but rather in a more traditional search for simplicity, inspiration, and humility. "At the end of the day, the people living in the house must be able to find more of themselves than of my intervention there. The role of that intervention is to be a permanent source of inspiration for the future."

Verwoordt was drawn to eastern philosophical traditions at a very young age. The inspiration he tapped into on his travels in Asia has stayed with him to this day, and is evident in much of his work. Respect for nature, the art of simplicity and harmony, the beauty found in humble objects, and the power of silence have woven their way into his designs, as has his personal interpretation of *wabi*,

▶▶▶

◀◀◀

an enlightened Japanese philosophy that values the beauty of imperfection, and the simplicity of things in their most natural state. As a result, intriguing contrasts between Asian and European styles, archaeology, and contemporary art are forged. "I'm inspired by art from all genres," he says, "from all parts of the world and from all sorts of periods. I like everything that is honest and real. *Arte povera*, for instance, the unsophisticated art of shepherds and monks from the mountains, was born from a great respect for nature. They were already making the most beautiful minimalistic objects hundreds of years ago. At the other end of the spectrum, the extreme sophistication of baroque might be chosen for effect, craftsmanship, or exuberance – but never to simply display riches."

One of Vervoordt's most significant works is the Kanaal Project in Antwerp, inspired by a desire to create an authentic cultural and residential island amid a wealth of art and nature. This former distillery and malting complex is being developed to be 'a city in the country', featuring apartments, lofts, and shops, as well as a home for the museum of the Axel & May Vervoordt Foundation. The original character of the historical site is being brought back to life in a striking example of Vervoordt's acknowledgment of time. "The 20th century was synonymous with production, consumption, and disposal," he says, "but now we are running low, both on places to dump waste and on forests to raid. In the 21st century, recuperation is playing a major role. In this way, the old becomes current again. We appreciate old walls, furniture that has not been restored, everything that in its original state has been transformed by time, the greatest sculptor of all. Time gives these materials a second skin. It's a gesture of love, a product of nature as transformed by human beings and the cosmos, which, over the years, has come to accept and integrate new forms. We must accept what nature and time have wrought." ■

Axel Vervoordt Kanaal, Stokerijstraat 15-19, 2110 Wijnegem
AXEL-VERVOORDT.COM

EVERYTHING THAT IN ITS ORIGINAL STATE HAS BEEN TRANSFORMED BY TIME, THE GREATEST SCULPTOR OF ALL.

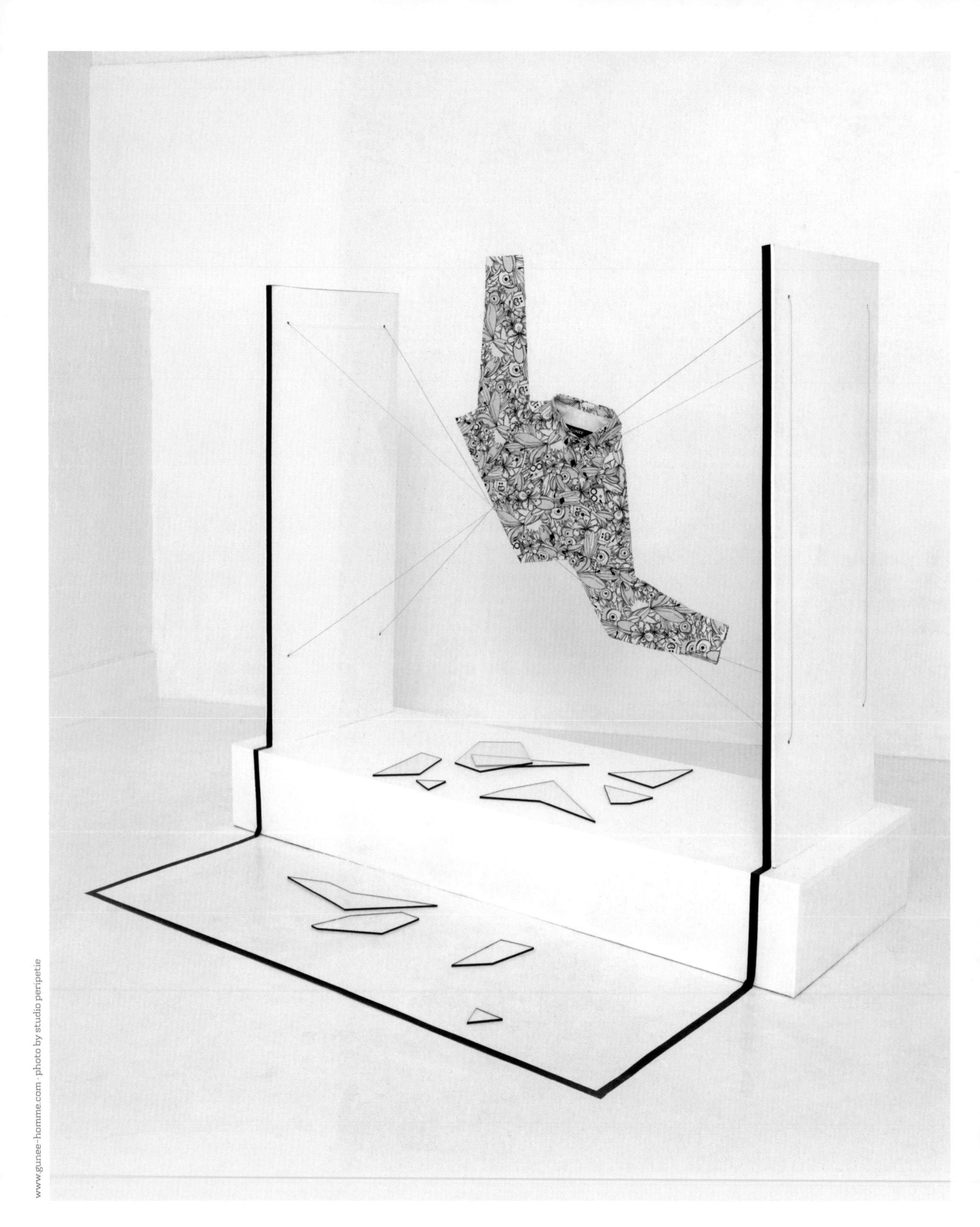
www.gunee-homme.com · photo by studio peripetie

GUNEE
HOMME

INTERLUDE

STYLE, CULTURE, & MISCELLANY

A GLOBAL SELECTION

CURATED

TIMEPIECES

Photos: *Mark Sanders* *Styling:* *Alison Elwin*

LAMBDA ROSÉGOLD
by NOMOS

Jacket by MHL
Top by RAG AND BONE
Trousers by MARGARET HOWELL

M40 IN BRUSHED STEEL
by UNIFORM WARES

Coat by COS
Roll neck by MARGARET HOWELL
Trousers by CALVIN KLEIN

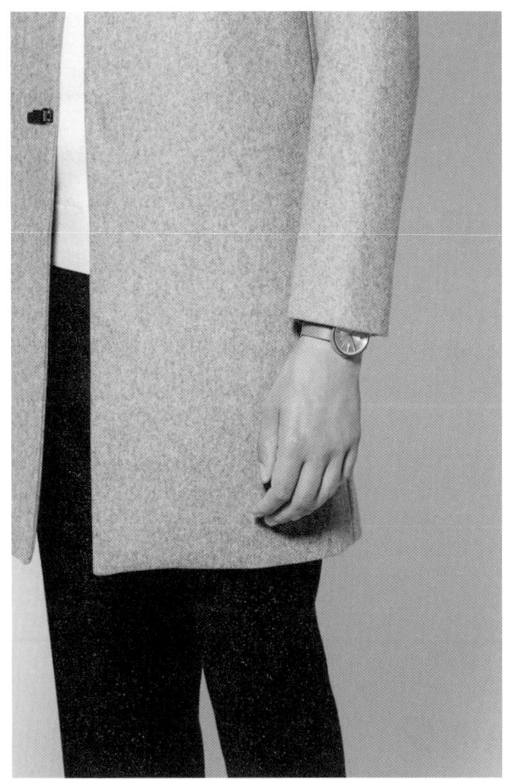

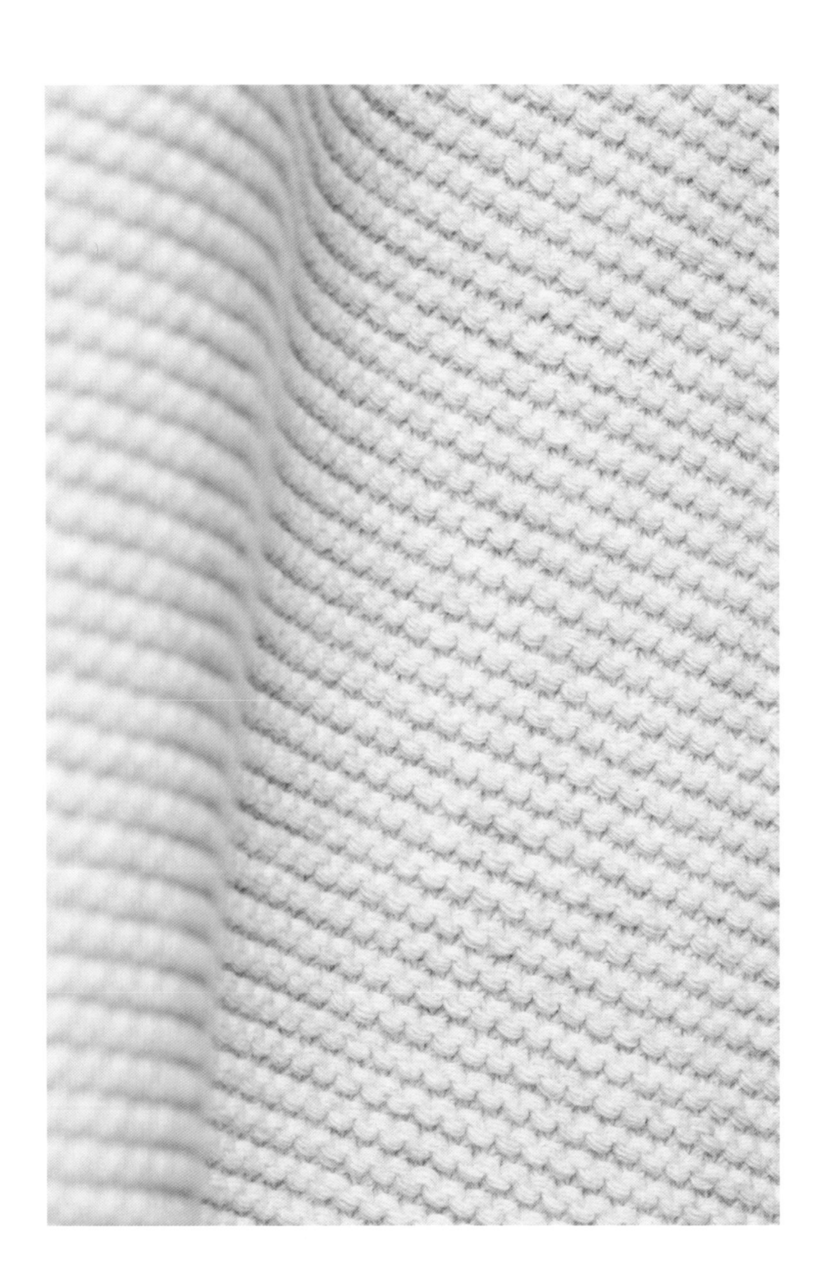

MAX BILL CHRONOSCOPE
by JUNGHANS

Jumper and trousers by COS
Shirt by SUNSPEL

EXPEDITION SCOUT
by TIMEX

Sweatshirt by ALBAM

KALLAN POCKET WATCH
by SKAGEN

INVISIBLE DESIGN

VITSOE FURNITURE

Words: *Lily Le Brun* *Photos:* *Rich Stapleton*

You might be surprised to discover that rather than business or design, Mark Adams, managing director of Vitsoe, studied zoology. "Biology excites me," he says. "At a detailed level, it's all about how an organism works, but at the macro level, you have to look at entire ecosystems. That's what makes me tick." Even more intriguingly, Adams does not view Vitsoe as a furniture company. "We are a service business that just happens to make some products," he explains. When you put these two pieces of information together, Vitsoe starts to make a lot more sense. "What you have inside here," he tells me as we walk around the company's Camden HQ, "is an ecosystem; a place where multiple details are constantly interacting."

Vitsoe makes and sells furniture designed exclusively by Dieter Rams, offering just three products; the *606 Universal Shelving System*, the *620 Chair Programme*, and the *621 Side Table*. Although widely considered design classics (the *606 Universal Shelving System* is in the permanent collection of the Museum of Modern Art in New York, and the *620 Chair Programme* is in the collections of both the V&A and the Design Museum), no two orders ever look quite the same. The emphasis at Vitsoe is on adaptability and longevity, not just outward appearances. The Vitsoe logo – the company's name in simple sans serif majuscule with a final ligature 'Œ' – is a rare sight at the Camden warehouse and office complex, and the product itself is deliberately anonymous. Adams likes to think of it as invisible furniture. "That's why people want it," he says, "because it is so self effacing. It provides a blank canvas against which your life can change and transform."

Adams recounts the story of a recent order received from a couple in New York. Both had been married before, and were about to move in together. Realising they both owned the off-white *606 Universal Shelving System*, they got back in touch with Vitsoe, who were able to easily merge the two systems to fit their new apartment. "This type of request happens all the time," he says, "few of us realise how much our lives are going to change." The system is designed to be "one of those increasingly rare things in your life that you can rely on for the rest of your life." The Vitsoe customer, according to Adams, is someone who "thinks beyond the end of their nose."

Vitsoe abides by Dieter Rams's 10 principles of good design, namely, that their products must be innovative, useful, aesthetically pleasing, understandable, unobtrusive, honest, long lasting, thorough, environmentally friendly, and have as little 'design' as possible. The *606 Universal Shelving System* consists of an aluminium E track, from which shelving, cabinets, and tables can be suspended. It is available in a limited number of sizes and colours, all depending on the needs of the customer. No tools are needed to assemble it, and the simplicity of the system means that the individual components can be rearranged and interchanged easily. The *620 Chair Programme,* a surprisingly comfortable, boxy leather chair, designed by Rams in 1962, also has flexibility and a long lifespan at its core. It swivels, connects up with others of its kind to make a sofa, and is easily reupholstered, when the time comes. The *621 Side Table*, dating from the same year, is simplicity itself; a discreet, injection moulded plastic side table, available in two colours and two sizes.

Dieter Rams and Niels Vitsoe met in 1957, when Rams was just 27 years old. The pair founded Vitsoe two years later in Frankfurt, with Rams continuing to work for electrical giant Braun, where he held the position of head of design from 1961 until 1995. In the early 1980s, a young Mark Adams made the decision to bail out of a well paid London headhunting job, going directly against his father's advice to keep furniture as a hobby. He became a shop assistant at a small West End design shop where he had first seen a Dieter Rams simple black shelving unit. Shortly after, the shop owners went bankrupt, and Adams, still in his early 20s, found himself looking around the wreckage, wondering what he could salvage. He decided to fly to Frankfurt for the weekend to introduce himself to Niels

▶▶▶

10 PRINCIPLES OF GOOD DESIGN ... INNOVATIVE, USEFUL, AESTHETICALLY PLEASING, UNDERSTANDABLE, UNOBTRUSIVE, HONEST, LONG LASTING, THOROUGH, ENVIRONMENTALLY FRIENDLY, AND WITH AS LITTLE 'DESIGN' AS POSSIBLE.

◀◀◀

Vitsoe, to whom he had only previously spoken on the phone, and returned from Germany with an agreement to import and sell Vitsoe furniture in the UK, where it was little known. Over the next seven years, he watched the company – still headed by an ageing Niels Vitsoe – falter. By 1993, it was in financial trouble, and Adams was invited to take a 51% stake in the business. Despite significant efforts, it was forced to close. Refusing to give up on the company, Adams shifted its entire manufacturing base to his home shores across the English Channel in 1995.

Since then, he has worked hard to streamline the business and make the design the best it can be. Every component is sourced from within the UK, and if something can be reused, it is. Even the cardboard packaging is cut to a specific size so that it can be returned to the warehouse and sent out again. The same goes for the product. Although the appearance of the shelving unit hasn't deviated from Rams's original, Adams tells me that it has undergone at least 90 changes since 1995. Today, every single order goes out worldwide directly from the Camden headquarters. "In many ways, we're becoming a small automotive business," Adams says, "buying in the best components from the best suppliers and then putting them together. They just happen to come out as furniture, rather than as a car." The company has an international team of planners who act as consultants and advisors to customers, as well as stores in London, New York City, Los Angeles, and Munich. Vitsoe furniture is not available to buy anywhere else, other than online, where they make the bulk of their sales. This direct approach has been integral to the regeneration of the company. "Our margins are under half the industry norm," Adams tells me. "The best way of being able to design well is to keep an intimacy with the customer. The minute you put in a middleman, all that honesty and integrity within the relationship breaks down."

Next year, Vitsoe are moving out of their increasingly cramped north London headquarters into a larger space in Leamington Spa in the West Midlands. The location has been carefully selected for its strong history of manufacturing and its close proximity to the UK's main rail freight terminal. Containers will be transported straight from trains to the port, and then onto ships bound for destinations across the world. The new building has been designed over many years with a quintessentially Vitsoe mindset; the system that lies behind it has been the priority. Conceived as a living experiment, it is also where Adams's long term goal of taking the business entirely into employee ownership will be realised.

In a world where short life cycles and inbuilt obsolescence have become the norm, Vitsoe is a reactionary force extending beyond furniture. "Vitsoe's purpose," Adams points out, "is to allow more people to live better, with less, that lasts longer. It's not about furniture or Rams. What Dieter and I talk about most of all is how Vitsoe moves beyond Dieter Rams and, possibly, beyond furniture completely." I ask if Vitsoe is more an ethos. "Absolutely" Adams replies. "There is a huge opportunity for us to change people's way of living and way of thinking. I think we are in a period of massive change, and the whole beauty of Vitsoe is that it will accommodate whatever the future throws at it." Adams's final words sum up not only this iconic brand, but also his relationship to it succinctly: "At Vitsoe, rather than guessing what the future holds, we just make sure we can adapt to change." ■

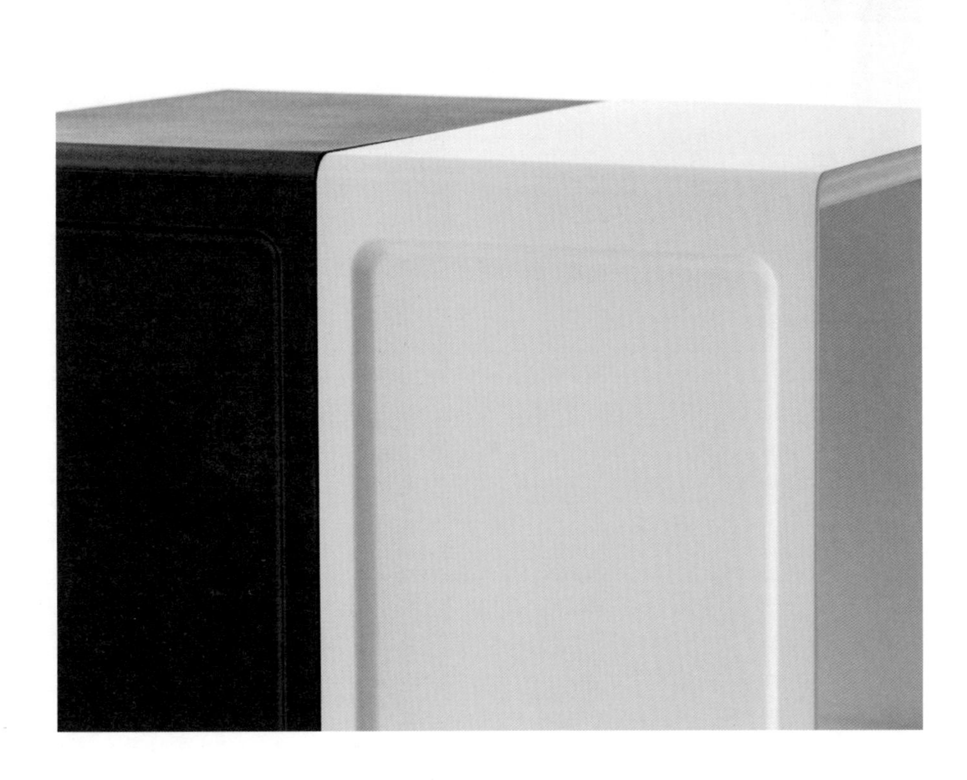

A UNIFORM VISION

A CONVERSATION WITH NORM ARCHITECTS

Words: *Justin H. Min* **Photos:** *Line Klein*

Norm Architects is more than simply an architecture studio; aside from an impressive portfolio of residential architecture work, the firm frequently engages in commercial interiors, industrial design, photography, graphics, and art direction. Co-founders Jonas Bjerre-Poulsen and Kasper Rønn do not see these varied channels as obstacles to a uniform vision, however. Instead, they focus on the advantages of functioning as a multidisciplinary design brand. "We gain a lot from engaging in such a wide range of disciplines," says Jonas. "When we are designing, for example, we think very much like architects, and we are very analytical. And because we also do interiors, the way we think about architectural landscapes is distinct from that of our colleagues; we think about the smaller details."

When Norm Architects was formally established in 2008, Jonas and Kasper had already been working together for over a decade in Copenhagen. These high school friends had been working at a petrol station and an institution for differently abled people, before ending up at the office of Danish designer Ole Palsby. "Kasper was there for five years; I was there for eight," says Jonas, "and that was where we got our informal education as designers."

Nods to Danish designers, such as Palsby and Poul Kjærholm, permeate the firm's distinct and highly acclaimed work. A prominent feature is Jonas and Kasper's use of geometric purity. "In all of our work, we start off with basic geometry – squares, circles, triangles. It's universally grounded, so the products that come out in the end are simple, yet appeal to everyone, regardless of their cultural influence," says Jonas. The architects also spend countless hours conceptualising the way light moves and feels within a space. "The amount of daylight coming into a space can create the right mood, and bring nature inside," says Jonas. "Our aim every time we begin a project is to create a space that feels warm, welcoming, and human, even before a single piece of furniture goes in. This is achieved through the way it's constructed, and how the materials feel."

Simplicity, clarity, and timelessness are values that resonate deeply. "When we started the company, we chose the name 'Norm' in order to go against what was in vogue. We wanted to do something that was based on established norms and standards that have

▸▸▸

◀◀◀

been refined for millennia," Jonas explains, "something that can stand the test of time, something we can be proud of in 10 or 20 years." In the digital age, where ideas and aesthetics are shared seamlessly and instantaneously, Jonas and Kasper strive toward universality, incorporating influences from across the globe. "Even though we are very influenced by traditional Japanese architecture, neither one of us has ever been to Japan," says Jonas. "Style and a sense of aesthetics is no longer connected to a specific region. It's not about being in a physical place anymore. Inspiration travels easily, so it's much more about taking ideas from all parts of the world."

The duo is working extensively with Scandinavian furniture and accessories brand Menu as designers and lead advisors. "Menu was one of the first companies we worked with as designers when we started in 2008," says Jonas of the partnership between the two firms. "We developed one product for them that became a huge success, and we continued to work with them until they approached us and asked if we wanted to be design directors for them." Upon accepting the position, Jonas and Kasper travelled the world in search of new collaborators, including both established design studios and young and emerging talent, who shared the same aesthetic vision for Menu's future trajectory. "In a relatively short time, we have completely rebranded the company and made a powerful statement in terms of Scandinavian design," says Jonas.

Paradoxically, the remarkable success of Norm Architects has prompted the company to downsize. While Norm once boasted 10 full time employees, the company now consists of only the two founding partners and Linda Korndal, head of architectural and interior projects. "There was a point when Kasper and I were spending all our time either in meetings, writing emails, or taking care of employees, and we looked forward to taking the weekends off," Jonas explains. "So we took a quick decision and decided to take on less, but to do it ourselves, and wake up every morning loving our jobs." The pair is now personally invested in each and every one of the studio's projects, with consistency across all their diverse undertakings. Jonas's home, having undergone multiple renovations whilst experimenting with new materials and techniques, is a testament to how his work is a joy and a hobby. "My home is a laboratory for new ideas. I need to look at things for a time and ask myself if it is still interesting after having lived with it for a couple of months," he says. "In order to do a really good job, I need to do something I love." ■

AGNES MARTIN

1912 – 2004

A RETROSPECTIVE

***Words:** Charlie Lee-Potter* ***Photos:** Rich Stapleton*

MINIMALISM ISN'T QUITE THE RIGHT WORD FOR THE RADIANT BEAUTY OF HER CANVASSES. IT IS IN THEIR RESTRAINT THAT THEIR FRAGILITY LIES, IN THEIR LUMINOSITY, THEIR RICHNESS, IN THEIR SLIGHT IMPERFECTIONS

With major retrospectives of the work of Barbara Hepworth, Sonia Delaunay, Marlene Dumas, and Agnes Martin, Tate is drawing our gaze back towards the great women artists of the 20th century. Even Tate, however, can be tremulous about articulating precisely what its grand plan is. At the launch of the Agnes Martin exhibition, Tate Modern's director, Chris Dercon, explained that, although recent shows of women artists have been important, "We don't want to re-write the history of art." Then, in a powerful intervention, the co-curator of the Martin show, Frances Morris, corrected him: "Actually, Chris – yes, we do." Along with fellow curator Tiffany Bell, she has designed a show that brings a new and powerful coherence to Martin's artistic trajectory. As assistant curator Dr Lena Fritsch points out, "Martin was a major artist. She was once photographed with the much younger, less influential artists Robert Indiana and Ellsworth Kelly. Martin was 10 years older than them, and she was so important, yet she's been forgotten by some people. This show is about reasserting her position."

It's perhaps appropriate that the tensions over women's contribution to contemporary art should be exposed via Agnes Martin and her own struggles. Her paintings embody tranquility – viewing a Martin painting is like listening to a long, slow exhalation of breath – but traces of torment are always present. The serenity for which she is famous was, according to Frances Morris, achieved through huge "personal and spiritual struggle." She was an important part of the vibrant New York art scene, and yet she opted for an unsettled life living in a pickup truck before moving to a solitary and isolated house in New Mexico. She was hugely ambitious, and yet she fought to see beyond ego. She sought beauty and serenity in her art, and yet frequent episodes of schizophrenia meant prolonged stays in hospital throughout the 1960s. After 1967, there followed a period when she didn't, or couldn't, paint at all. "She stopped painting for seven years", says Lena Fritsch. "She was schizophrenic and, on the one hand, she meditated and dealt with it, but in the 1960s, she had serious psychiatric episodes and was hospitalised repeatedly. She's very difficult to understand. Her mind is very complex – there are meditative and Zen influences, yet she was struggling with mental illness. She saw some works in her head and they were very small. She then made calculations to render them as much larger pieces."

For the seven years that she didn't paint, Martin "wrote a lot and that's very important in the exhibition", says Lena Fritsch. "The words are very typically Agnes Martin – very reduced, very spare." In fact, Martin's words are so pared back as to be more aphorism than conversation. She became known for statements such as "My paintings have neither objects nor space nor time nor anything," and, "Beauty is the mystery of life. It is not just in the eye. It is in the mind. It is our positive response to life." Works that are so apparently simple and reduced inevitably ask a great deal of the viewer, as do her terse written instructions.

▶▶▶

UNTITLED #5 (1998)

Kunstsammlung Nordrhein-Westfalen, Düsseldorf

MORNING (1965)

Tate

◄◄◄

According to Fritsch, however, it's important not to feel bullied by Martin's own interpretations. "Her writing is very beautiful and focusses on innocence, but I don't see Agnes Martin's words as an explanation of her work, more as an artwork in themselves. I don't let her dictate to me. Someone once called her an 'art nun', but it's not that simple. As a curator, you have to find a balance between what an artist wants and says, and what we see in the work for ourselves."

Agnes Martin certainly did her best to circumvent the controlling gaze of her audience. She was a serial destroyer of her own art. "Having thought about it carefully," says Fritsch, "we decided not to include any works that she herself didn't see as part of her *oeuvre*." Even in her 90s, commuting to her studio from lodgings in an assisted living facility, Martin was still meticulous about destroying work that she didn't think represented her vision. Her art dealer and friend Arne Glimcher said that one morning, just before she died, he visited her and she "beckoned me to come closer to the bed. 'There are three new paintings in the studio. The one on the wall is finished and the two on the floor need to be destroyed.' Would I go to the studio and destroy them for her? This was her last request."

One of the many difficulties when collating work for a major Agnes Martin exhibition is that the life that resonates from the original canvasses is stifled when the works are reproduced photographically. "When we started collecting possible images for inclusion, we found that there are so many works simply called *Untitled*. It was very difficult to see them properly when we were sent photocopies of them," Lena Fritsch says. "Colour reproduction of her paintings is so hard to get right. It's very difficult to reproduce them and keep their spirit. They can often seem a little pale and flat." The originals are anything but. The pencil lines of Martin's characteristic grids that, at a distance, seem so regimented, display occasional tremours and fluctuations, as though Martin was taking a breath or was momentarily distracted. The all too human frailty of Martin herself is written in those almost perfect lines. Again, up close, the apparently flat pastel pinks and dilute greys of her canvasses radiate a gentle haze in which the hand and spirit of the artist is all too apparent. The pieces themselves are of uniform size, but even here, Martin herself is present. "She repeatedly chose canvasses of 72" by 72"," says Frances Morris. "At six foot by six foot, they are just slightly bigger than her body, but each one still holds the idea of her human reach in the world." As Martin grew older and frailer, she reduced their sizes correspondingly; her final works were produced on canvasses of 60" by 60", a poignant reminder of her failing power and energy. For those who curate Agnes Martin's work, there is always one question in particular that must be asked of those from whom the paintings are borrowed: Are they willing to lend their works without glass? To trap a Martin painting behind glass is to imprison the radiant haze emanating from it. "We were very lucky," says Morris. "We managed to persuade most people to lend their work to us unglazed."

A natural divide in the show corresponds to those intervening seven years when Martin stopped painting, and work from the period up to 1967 is exhibited in galleries without natural daylight. It's in these early rooms that we find Martin's radiant, almost ostentatious work *Friendship* (1963), rendered in rich, luminous incised gold leaf. To mark the beginning of the phase when Martin stopped painting, we are led down a narrow corridor where Martin's series of 1973 screenprints, titled as a group as *On a Clear Day*, are displayed. It's in this connecting passageway that Martin exhorts us to find innocence of mind: "If you can go with them and hold your mind as empty and tranquil as they are and recognise your feelings at the same time, you will realise your full response to this work." In a piece of proto-Freudian stage management, we are taken from this narrow corridor and delivered into rooms lit by daylight, where we find Martin's characteristic late work. As Frances Morris puts it, after Martin's mixed media experiments of the late 1950s with bottle tops, wood, spikes, and found objects, and her extraordinarily lavish and rich gold painting of 1963, "it's as though she's taking the ego out of her work." It would be logical to argue that, having excised her ego, Agnes Martin had succeeded in becoming the kind of minimalist some believe her to be. Ultimately, however, minimalism isn't quite the right word for the radiant beauty of her canvasses. It is in their restraint that their fragility lies, in their luminosity, their richness, in their slight imperfections, their humanity. ■

Mont Jura
Noir Mont
la grande Combe
DEP. du DOUBS
VALLEE de JOUX
les Charbonnieres
le Pont
Lac Ter
Fontaine des Alemans
Combe-noir
l'Abbaye
le Sentier
Chenit
Berolle
SUN
MON
TUE
WED
THU
FRI
SAT

HAUTE HORLOGERIE

AUDEMARS PIGUET: MASTER WATCHMAKERS

Words: *Justin H. Min* ***Photos:*** *Adrienne Pitts*

Ami Louis Meylan arrives each day at the Audemars Piguet workshop in a suit, white shirt, tie, and black hat. Once stationed at his workbench, he replaces his jacket with a lab coat. He works as a *repasseur*, tasked with making the final adjustments to a movement's mechanism. During the brief moments of respite from his horological handiwork, he gazes out of the window to the horizon beyond. The facility is bathed in light, and enveloped by lush forests and emerald pastures amid the vast mountainous backdrop of the Vallée de Joux. Although a century lapsed between the founding of the Audemar Piguet Company and the moment Meylan first fixed his watchmaker's loupe into his eye, the company and the extensive pedigree of its master watchmakers remain largely unchanged.

The villagers of Le Brassus possess the perfect alchemy for a thriving watchmaking industry; time, quiet, patience, and ingenuity. This small settlement in the Jura Mountains in western Switzerland, with its harsh climate and poor soil, was noted for ushering in the first wave of industrial activity in the Vallée de Joux. The village soon became known for its technical precision, and transformed itself into the cradle of *haute horlogerie*. Geneva watchmakers came to depend on the complex movements manufactured here.

It was here, among the finest watchmakers in the world, that 22 year old Jules Louis Audemars and 24 year old Edward Auguste Piguet founded Audemars Piguet in 1875, with a workshop in the family home, a registered trademark, and a partnership contract valid for a decade. The partnership continues to this day, and Audemars Piguet is the oldest fine watchmaker to remain in the hands of its founding families. Jasmine Audemars, the company's current chairwoman, is the great granddaughter of Jules Louis, and several other members of the Audemars clan still sit on the board.

Combining traditional craft with modern technological exactitude, Audemars Piguet handcrafts each of its 32,000 watches per year, with their most extensively produced models never exceeding 1,000 units each. As one of three major Swiss watch producers, the brand finds itself in the rarefied company of Patek Philippe and Vacheron Constantin, while Tiffany & Co. and Cartier use Audemars Piguet movements to this day.

Although the company has acquired two additional production sites in Le Locle and Meyrin-Geneva, the vast majority of design, production, and assembly of Audemars Piguet timepieces still takes place at its 11,000 m² Le Brassus headquarters. The facility's understated

▶▶▶

◄◄◄

interiors and protective sound barriers keep disturbances to a minimum as design and development teams work in concert over the course of three to five years to turn an idea into a functioning horological artwork. Cases, straps, dials, hands, and winding crowns all begin life as sketches, and are reworked over and again until the perfect blend of form and function is achieved. Computer designers and art directors then collaborate to transform the sketches into more concrete visions on screen, working with precise dimensions and specifications until a prototype can be produced.

The Le Brassus workshops, where master craftsmen sit meticulously polishing, bevelling, and decorating, feature huge, two metre high windows looking out over an immaculate view of the Orbe River valley, and letting in soft northern light. It is, perhaps, this well known harmony with nature that has led to conjecture that the quality of an Audemars Piguet chime is partly due to tempering steel gongs in horse urine, and that their movements are lubricated with the purest drops of oil. Once the individual components of the movement have been scrupulously manufactured and finished, a single watchmaker is tasked with assembling the several hundred parts over the course of two to three months. With surgeon like precision, the watchmaker starts by putting certain components together, testing them, and then taking them apart again to hone or polish given sections – such as correcting the tooth of a gear by 100th of a millimetre – until a satisfactory result is obtained. The watch's final adjustments are made through a variable series of tests to ensure regularity and accuracy, then the dial is added, the hands are attached, the mechanism is anchored to the case, and a strap is finally affixed.

It takes around six months for an Audemars Piguet timepiece to come into being, and this is only after years of designing, conceptualising, and prototyping. To don a *Royal Oak* or *Millenary* is to wear a piece of history. It is the result of generations acquiring the finer points of their trade, sitting at the same workbenches, fixing their watchmaker's loupes to their eyes, and holding the same tools in their hands. As Simon Van Booy once wrote, "Actually, years mean nothing. It's what's inside them." As far as Audemars Piguet is concerned, what's inside is 140 years of uninterrupted excellence. ■

READING ROOM

THE PERFECT NOOK

Photos: *Anders Schonnemann* *Styling:* *Nathalie Schwer*

READING ROOM CREDITS

PAGE 135

Book table, vintage, ***Fil de Fer***
Marble balls, ***Broste***
Vase, ***Georg Jensen***
Print, Haze, ***Anne Nowak***
Armchair, ***by Lassen***

PAGE 136

Candle holders, ***Broste***
Table, ***Muuto***
Lamp, ***Anour***
Marble ball, ***Broste***
Pouf, ***Muuto***
Blanket, ***Broste***

PAGE 137

Book table, vintage, ***Fil de Fer***
Lamp, ***Kroyer - Saetter - Lassen***
Lounge chair, ***Gubi***

PAGE 138-139

Statue, vintage, ***Fil de Fer***
Vase, Haberli, ***Georg Jensen***
Print, ***Anne Nowak***
Couch by Greta Grossmann, ***Gubi***
Vintage lamp, ***Fil de Fer***
Bauhaus bar wagon, ***Please wait to be seated***
Coffee press, ***Muuto***

ARTIST SERIES: CEREAL *collaborations*

NO. is a respected New York based ceramics brand, loved for its simplicity and elegance. We've partnered with them to deliver a unique, collaborative collection.

We worked closely with Romy Northover, the force behind the brand, to create a series of pieces that focusses on 'beauty in function and form.' Our inspiration was drawn from various cultures, including modern Scandinavian and traditional Japanese.

Words: *Lucy Brook* *Photos:* *Carmen Chan*

This collection is available to purchase at ***shop.readcereal.com***

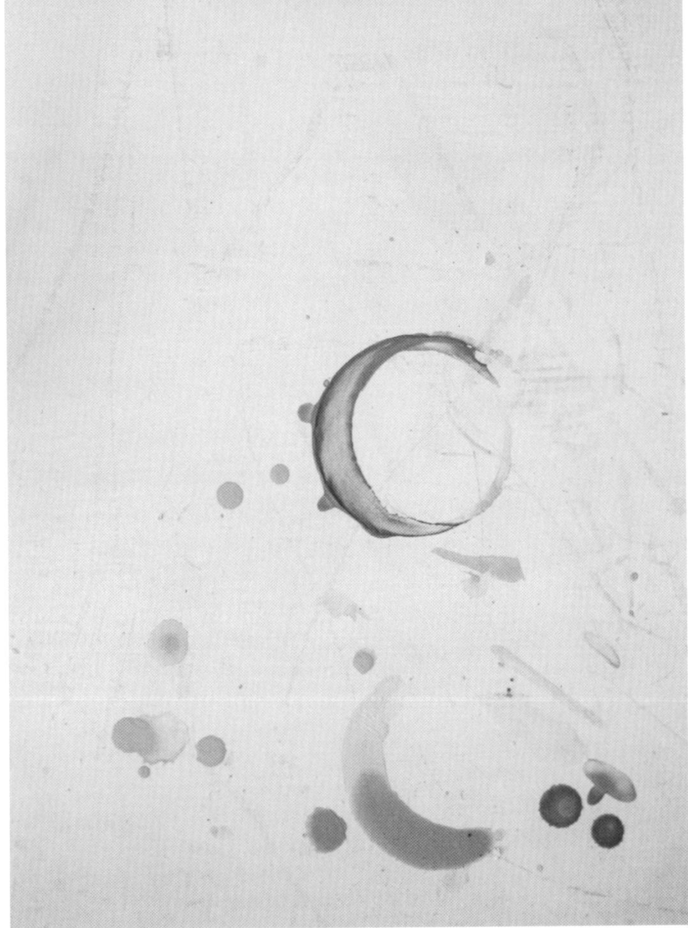

NICOLE PATEL

Nicole Patel is a Nyack based artist specialising in beautifully serene minimalist grids on various mediums, including canvas, plaster, beeswax, and Italian marble.

The subtle pieces made exclusively for *Cereal* are crafted from muslin and paper with a gradient of Japanese Merino wool threads. The thread gives the pieces an organic softness that Patel says is "very easy to live with".

Words: Sean Hotchkiss Photos: Justin Chung

This series is available to purchase at ***shop.readcereal.com***

PANAMA CITY

PANAMA

9°05'59.4"N, 79°24'18.0"W

PANAMA CANAL

CONNECTING OCEANS

Words: *Richard Aslan* *Photos:* *Kate Holstein*

A flank of blue steel arms whirr as they load containers, bright as children's building blocks, onto the great vessels churning the soupy waters of Bahía de Limón. Moving cargo from the Atlantic to the Pacific through the Panama Canal is still the work of thousands – though few backs and thighs are strained with heavy lifting any more. Instead, workers drive forklifts and artics through the walled in depots of Coco Solo and Colón Free Trade Zone, and along the service roads flanking the concrete headland of Nuevo Cristobál. The ships, sea water rusting spots in their painted skins, plough past them west, then south into a great inlet, migrating along invisible trenches dug from the sea floor.

They advance through waterlogged hills, giant interlopers on the land, each kilometre of their journey paid for in prodigious loss of human life. The combined might of malaria, yellow fever, and neglect carried more than 25,000 to their graves, the vast majority during the first doomed attempt to dig across the isthmus by the French. From 1882, the goldrush boomtown of Gatún, 15 km inland and briefly renamed Cité de Lesseps, was the epicentre of Ferdinand Marie, Comte de Lesseps' operation. By the end of the century, however, the half finished trenches had fallen silent, and the reputation of the *Grand Français*, feted for his other canal in Suez, was in tatters. Undone by wet earth, an outraged press, and the clamour of 800,000 ruined investors, he narrowly avoided imprisonment, not for charges of manslaughter, but rather bribery and corruption.

Theodore Roosevelt took up the cause of the unfinished canal in one of his first presidential speeches in 1901. "No single great work which remains to be undertaken on this continent," he bristled, from behind monocle and moustaches, "is

▶▶▶

R43
MAERSK
R46

as of such consequence to the American people." When the Colombian government failed to show sufficient enthusiasm for his plans for their isthmian province, Washington turned instead to the Panamanian independence movement. In November 1903, the gunboat *Nashville* sliced, sleek and white, into the bay at Colón in a pointed show of strength in support of its *protégé*. In return, the nascent Panamanian state granted its powerful northern neighbour a wedge of rainforest 16 km wide and 80 km long 'as though it were sovereign' to complete their canal where the French had failed, and thereafter administer it 'in perpetuity'. Even the purse of a superpower was strained by the costs, with a 10 million USD purchase price for the land, 250,000 USD in annual rent, almost as much again to quieten the outrage in Bogotá, and another 40 million USD for French assets on the ground.

Despite presidential orders to "make dirt fly", excavation progressed with agonising slowness. The Isthmian Canal Commission, meticulous in its duty to avoid a re-run of French catastrophes, held Chief Engineer Findlay hostage with an insistence on checks, double checks, and unanimous approval for every decision. Recruitment drives in Jamaica met with hostility; the memories of French abuses were still fresh, and vast inequalities in the treatment of black and white workers remained unaddressed. After the first Bucyrus steam shovel sputtered into action, chomping at huge mouthfuls of earth, celebration quickly gave way to frustration when the rusting Panama Railroad proved incapable of carrying away the spoils. The threat of another failure to link two oceans loomed over the stubborn piles of dirt like storm clouds. Chief Medical Officer Gorgas had more success. Convinced by the then outlandish notion that the ubiquitous swarms of mosquitoes were not only a nuisance, but also carried malaria and yellow fever, he won Roosevelt's approval to increase his mosquito brigades from 200 to 2,000, and fumigated Aëdes aegypti into oblivion. Wholesale deaths from yellow fever finally halted when Gorgas spent 90,000 USD on copper mosquito screening. It took a new chief engineer, John Stevens, to get the excavations moving again with workers' welfare and fixing the railroad as his priorities.

Plans to use brute force to plough across the isthmus at sea level weren't abandoned until late 1905. Instead, ships purpose built to a maximum of 289.56 m from stern to bow and 32.31 m across the beam now glide into the twin channels at Gatún locks, their flanks all but grazing the sides. Three chambers employ more than 300,000 m^3 of water, taking more than three hours to raise the craft the necessary 26 m to the Gatún Dam. This vast earthwork was completed in 1907, and it took another six years for the valleys behind it to be engulfed by the slowly rising waves, creating what was, at the time, the biggest manmade body of water on the planet. Vessels trace a cautious path across an improbable blue surface over submerged peaks and forests, each ponderous change in direction leading them finally to Culebra Cut. This terraced valley, site of endless landslides, cuts its way through the highest terrain on the canal route and is named for the mountain that was blasted away with over 27,000 tonnes of dynamite to create it. Its end marks the beginning of the descent back to sea level, the blue horizon of the Pacific in sight beyond Pedro Miguel and Miraflores locks.

The black and red hull of the *SS Ancon*, loaded with cement, made the first official passage to great fanfare on August 15, 1914, almost 45 years after the idea of the canal was first taken seriously. 'In perpetuity', meanwhile, expired on 31 December 1999, the handover of the canal ending decades of tension, increasing militarisation, and unrest. With the passing years, as the number of vessels using the waterway had multiplied, the proportion of the world's commercial fleet too large to pass through the locks also swelled. In 2007, the Panamanian government busied itself with the largest excavations since works began almost a century before, and the newly broadened channels are all but complete. Each time a ship is disgorged into the final dogleg stretch of bay, the suburbs of Panama City spreading out to the east, it tells a story underscored by the sweat of tens of thousands of labourers, recruited from all over the Caribbean and as far afield as Spain and Italy. It is a story of power, money, soil, and steel. ■

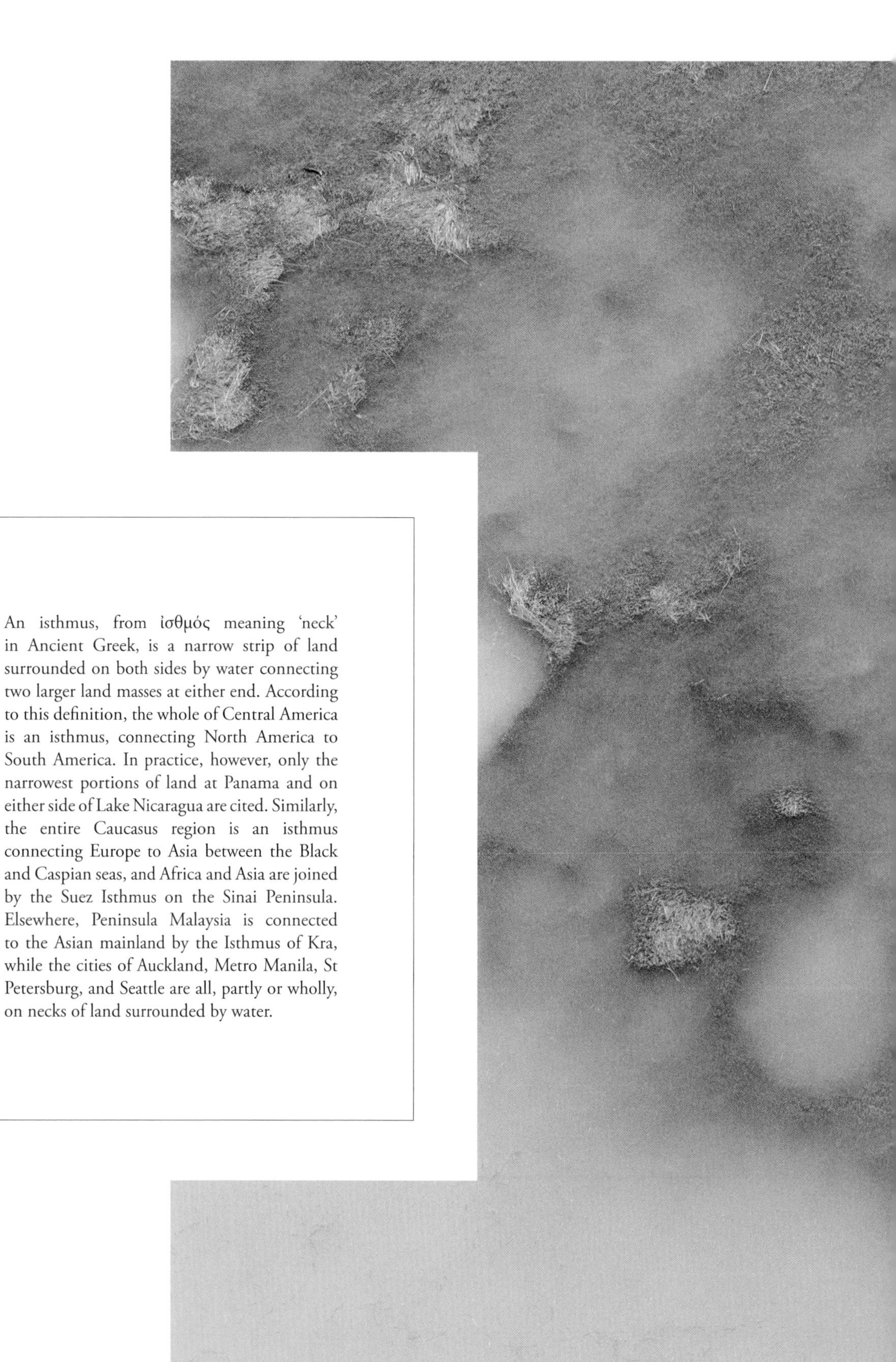

An isthmus, from ἰσθμός meaning 'neck' in Ancient Greek, is a narrow strip of land surrounded on both sides by water connecting two larger land masses at either end. According to this definition, the whole of Central America is an isthmus, connecting North America to South America. In practice, however, only the narrowest portions of land at Panama and on either side of Lake Nicaragua are cited. Similarly, the entire Caucasus region is an isthmus connecting Europe to Asia between the Black and Caspian seas, and Africa and Asia are joined by the Suez Isthmus on the Sinai Peninsula. Elsewhere, Peninsula Malaysia is connected to the Asian mainland by the Isthmus of Kra, while the cities of Auckland, Metro Manila, St Petersburg, and Seattle are all, partly or wholly, on necks of land surrounded by water.

CASCO VIEJO

HEART OF A CITY

Words: *Lily Le Brun* *Photos:* *Kate Holstein*

Panama City, perched where oceans kiss and the Americas shake hands, has a phoenix like past. Founded in 1519 by Spanish *conquistadores*, it survived slave rebellion, earthquake, and devastating flames, before being razed to the ground a century and a half later by pirates. Fleeing inhabitants established themselves anew on a nearby, more easily defendable peninsula, at the mouth of a river that, centuries later, became the entrance to the Panama Canal. This town, known today simply as the Casco Viejo, or Casco Antiguo, rose from the ashes to become one of the richest and most densely populated neighbourhoods in the Americas.

Panama City grew up around this neighbourhood, which remained at the epicentre of Panamanian life. It was where the grand houses and the government buildings were, and, in 1917, during the heady years following the completion of the Panama Canal, where the city's first 'skyscraper' was built. Designed by one of Panama's most celebrated architects of the time, Leonardo Villanueva Meyer, and commissioned by the American Trade Development Company, the six storey building – known as the American Trade Building – was the first to be made using reinforced concrete, with techniques perfected during the canal's construction. Its elegant neoclassical design contained state of the art residencies, as well as a popular department store. As the century progressed, however, many of the area's wealthier residents began moving out to the suburbs. The elegant plazas crumbled, and stately buildings were inhabited by weeds, squatters, and stray dogs. Scaffolding propping up pockmarked walls became permanent, and trees grew tall in former ballrooms.

By 2000, the American Trade Building was the graffiti strewn outpost of one of the area's many street gangs, who used its superior vantage point to assert control over their territory. Ramón Arias, a former lawyer who had recently become involved in restoration projects, knew the building well; his great, great grandfather, Ramón Arias Feraud, had commissioned it. "It stood as a forgotten landmark in the middle of one of the most important plazas in the Old City," Arias remembers. Once again, Panama City was embarking on a cycle of regeneration, so in 2007, Arias added the American Trade Building to his list of projects. "It only seemed right to restore the building," he says. "The Casco Viejo needed a hotel."

The Casco Viejo was made a UNESCO World Heritage site in 1997, two years before the USA finally ceded power over the canal and its surrounding territories to the Panamanian government. Economically, the city had begun to flourish once more, and the road was open for its oldest neighbourhood to revive its reputation as one of the most beautiful Spanish colonial cities in the world. Arias is a founding partner of Conservatorio, a real estate company that restores buildings across the Casco Viejo. While swathes of Panama City have been taken over by bland new building developments, Conservatorio has been working hard to restore historic houses in the district, while maintaining its bustling diversity. As well as hotels, shops, and luxury apartments, they also develop affordable housing for the residents of this traditionally working class neighbourhood.

▶▶▶

AMERICAN TRADE HOTEL

This page INTERIOR GREENERY
Opposite ROOM DETAILS

acehotel.com/panama

A resident of Casco for 23 years, Arias says the main challenge for the company has been "preserving the old, while creating a vibrant neighbourhood with its own particular flavours, and maintaining a balance for all groups of society to feel a part of it." Arias's co-founder at Conservatorio is K C Hardin, a North American who witnessed the quick transformation of South Beach in Miami and Williamsburg in New York. "They were exciting times," he told the *Financial Times* in 2012, "but the trouble with gentrification is the displacement of the culture and the community which drew people there in the first place. The maintenance of human architecture – that's what we are trying to achieve here."

In 2013, American Trade Hotel opened. Arias, who remains a joint owner, says that preserving the old structure of the American Trade Building was always a priority. From the very beginning, the restoration was "a dialogue between the building's past, its history, and its new use as a hotel." Its white stucco exterior reflects past grandeur, while its interiors have been updated with the clean lines of mid century furniture and understated contemporary colour, punctuated by graphic tiles and bright textiles.

The new hotel was a collaborative effort between Conservatorio, Commune Design, and Atelier Ace, the creative team behind the global chain of boutique hotels. Alongside the American Trade Building they also worked on a cluster of additional historic buildings, all at the centre of the Casco Viejo. These buildings nurture a sense of the historical importance of the city as an intersection of culture, business, and ecology. The American Trade Hall, a large event space, occupies a building that was originally a branch of the National City Bank of New York – one of the financiers of the Panama Canal – and is modelled after its headquarters in downtown Manhattan. Danilo's Jazz Club hosts local talent and international musicians. Café Unido uses only coffee from the surrounding area – something of a novelty in this city, despite the quality of the local crop.

In the shadow of the American Trade Hotel, museums, up market restaurants, luxury condos, and boutiques are increasingly taking up residence beneath the well weathered red roofs that populate the peninsula. Yet the uniformity that often accompanies gentrification still feels a long way off. Defined by its massive sea wall, built to defend the city from further pirate attacks, the Casco Viejo is small; just three avenues hem in the irregular blocks of buildings that have grown organically over four centuries. The layout of the neighbourhood – a contained, complex grid of streets wending their way down to the sea – has remained largely unchanged since the 1680s. It evokes a bohemian atmosphere, with bright flowers flowing over balconies, sun bleached murals adorning crumbling stucco walls, music seeping from doorways, and street vendors hawking Panama hats under large, rainbow coloured umbrellas.

Despite the growth of tourism and ubiquitous construction, poverty still haunts the old heart of Panama, and the work of conservation is far from complete. Change is clearly afoot, but the multiplicity of worlds contained within this mesh of narrow streets reflects the area's historic role. It has always been a junction, and a site for the exchange of ideas, culture, and ambition – it is this that has given the area its vitality. The international team involved in the restoration of the Casco Viejo reflects the Spanish, French, African, Caribbean, and US influences that can all be found within its streets. Like the neighbourhood itself, the American Trade Hotel bears the scars of decades of decay superimposed over the self confidence of the years following the construction of the canal. "Preserving Casco", Arias says, "reminds us of our history and our humanity."

SOBERANÍA NATIONAL PARK

AN ACCESSIBLE RAINFOREST

Words: Justin H. Min **Photos:** *Kate Holstein*

25 km north of Panama City, on the eastern shore of the Panama Canal, lie 222 km² of dense tropical rainforest. This is Soberanía National Park, a pristine landscape of undulating hills and steep slopes decked in clusters of lush *cuipos*, lianas, and royal palms. Established in 1980, the park stretches from Limón to Lago Gatún, and is home to more than 1,300 varieties of plant and over 100 different mammal species. The Pipeline Road, initially constructed for pipeline maintenance during WWII, also attracts avid birdwatchers from across the world, regularly flocking to the area in the hope of catching a rare glimpse of one the shyer representatives of the 525 avian species found here. Visitors can also walk the Las Cruces Trail, dating back to the 16th century when it was used by Spanish *conquistadores* to carry Peruvian gold across the isthmus. This is no remote wilderness, however; at just a 40 minute drive from the city, Soberanía National Park is one of the most accessible rainforests in the world.

CEREAL
VIEW CART (0)
MAGAZINE
JOURNAL
CITY GUIDES
GALLERY
SHOP
CEREAL

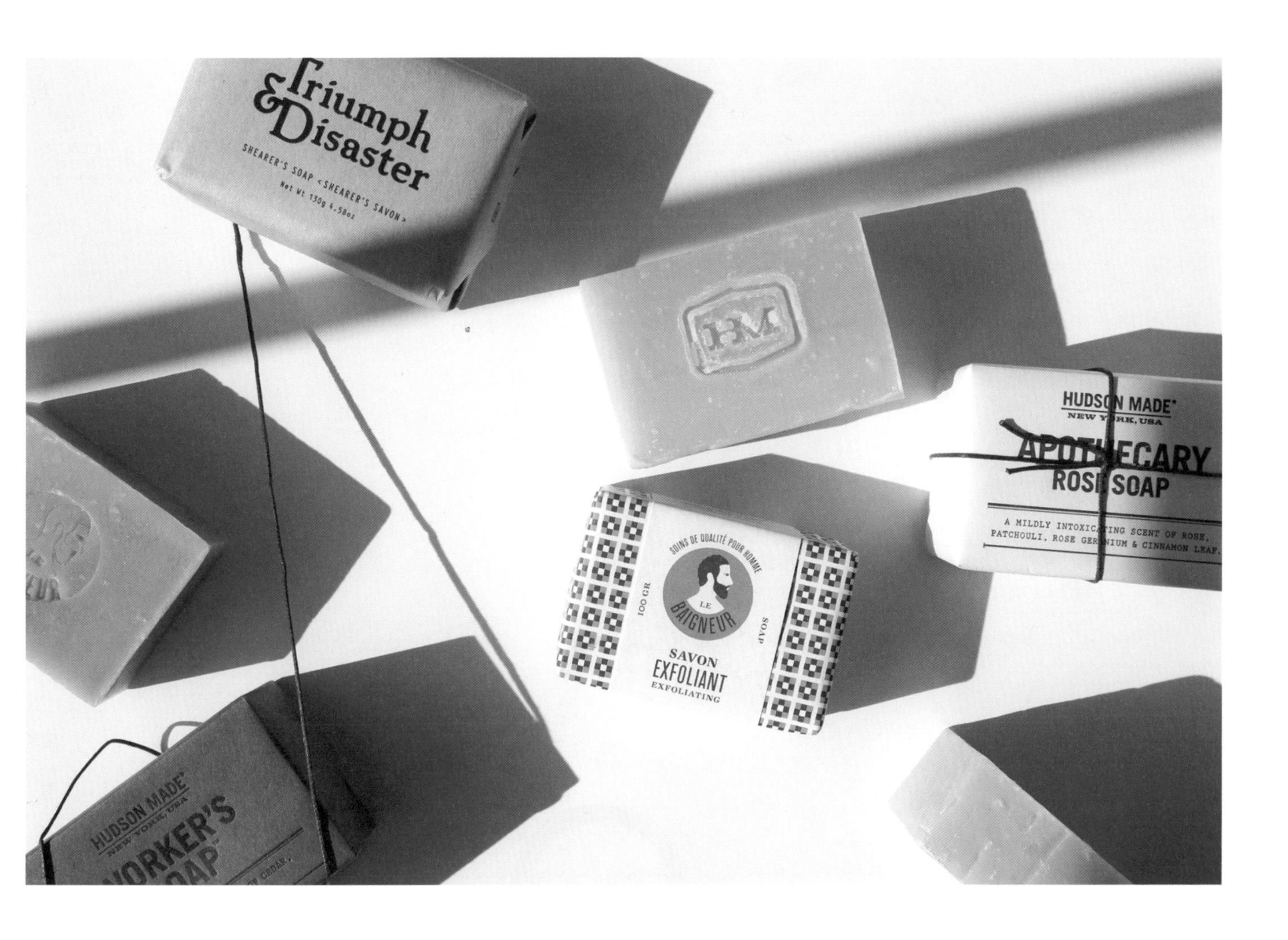
Triumph & Disaster
SHEARER'S SOAP <SHEARER'S SAVON>
HM
HUDSON MADE
NEW YORK, USA
ROSE SOAP
SOINS DE QUALITÉ POUR HOMME
LE BAIGNEUR
100 GR
SOAP
SAVON
EXFOLIANT
EXFOLIATING
HUDSON MADE
NEW YORK, USA

CEREAL

TRAVEL & STYLE